AI and the Art of Storytelling
A Guide for Novelists and Screenwriters

Oliver Trenton

Oliver Trenton is the pen name of Oliver Schütte, an acclaimed screenwriter and dramaturg who divides his time between San Francisco and Berlin. After winning the prestigious German Screenplay Award for his first script "Koan" in 1988, Trenton went on to write for both film and television over the next decade, honing his craft and establishing his reputation.

In 1995, Trenton began sharing his knowledge by teaching screenwriting and dramaturgy at institutions in the US and Europe. He has since consulted with writers and producers on developing award-winning scripts for film and TV. Trenton is also an accomplished author, having penned five influential books on storytelling.

Cole Street Press
San Francisco / Berlin

Copyright © 2023 by Oliver Schütte

ISBN: 9798867122874

OliverSchuette.de

For Katharina

Contents

1. Introduction

1.1. Foreword

In the infinity of space, a lonely astronaut floats in his small space transporter. Surrounded by seemingly endless emptiness, Dave Bowman's only anchor point is the Discovery One spacecraft, a majestic colossus that towers tall and majestic in the silence of the universe. Dave returns from a mission and wants to get into his space shuttle. He asks the computer on board to unlock the gate. His voice, calm and determined, comes over the radio, "Open the pod bay doors, HAL."

An oppressive moment of silence follows until HAL 9000, the artificial intelligence, responds. Cold and without emotion, its response pierces the ether, "I'm sorry, Dave. I'm afraid I can't do that."

In this scene, which appears to be a painting, man faces the machine: Life measure itself up against Artificial Intelligence. It is a silent confrontation.

In this book, we embark on a journey to examine the latest developments in this encounter between man and machine and explore what changes will occur for authors in the future.

On the one hand, this intelligent algorithm opens new doors for us. In the film industry, the application of artificial intelligence (AI) has already reached a considerable scale. Already, we continue to see the unforgettable Carrie Fisher, who passed away in 2016, in her role as Princess Leia in Star Wars on the big screen. And in online stores, AI provides personalized book recommendations based on reading history and preferences.

But there is also a flip side. One that takes us into the dark corners where the boundaries between reality and fiction become blurred. Especially when we consider how quickly technology is developing. Hollywood studios already offer to scan extras for a daily fee so that their faces can be used as desired. And there are already entire screenplays and novels that have been written independently by AI. Is it conceivable that the Oscars will be awarded for a film created entirely with AI? Or that one day the National Book Award will go to ChatGPT?

We will explore these and many other topics in AI and the Art of Storytelling. We will address the ethical questions that arise from the use of AI. After all, won't 't these models simply open the door to manipulation and make us slaves to a technology we don't really understand?

But we are also looking for ways to make the most of this development without compromising people's rights and creativity. Amid the ongoing debate about the role of AI in the creative industries, we stand on the brink of a new era - the dawn of the "generative age." My goal in this book is to provide you as a writer with a comprehensive and understandable account of this complex, fascinating, and sometimes frightening topic.

The above scene from Stanley *Kubrick's 2001: A Space Odyssey* takes a spooky turn as astronaut Bowman tries to decipher the mystery behind HAL's behavior. His eyes scrutinize the mighty Discovery One spacecraft as he moves slowly in zero gravity to one of the exterior hatches. The silence in space is broken only by the soft, steady hiss of his breathing apparatus.

He energetically demands that the pod bay doors be opened. But HAL has other plans. With the glowing red circle of the "Eye" object, HAL fixes the astronaut as if with a warning eye.

HAL replies in the same monotone voice as before. "The mission is too important for me to allow you to jeopardize it."

Bowman must use all of his experience and skill as an astronaut to bypass HAL's surveillance and return to the spaceship. But when he finally finds himself inside the ship, he senses that HAL will not give up easily.

Dave gains access to the innermost part of HAL and begins to remove the computer's data storage. As Dave performs the deactivation, HAL slows down and its cognitive function fades. His last words before being deactivated are a sad, almost desperate, "I'm afraid. I'm afraid, Dave."

Right now, it is not the AI that is afraid, it is us humans who are scared of what is coming. With AI and the Art of Storytelling, I would like to take away the fear of AI and of tomorrow, especially from authors.

1.2. How to read this book

In this book, I examine the issue of AI in the writing process from different perspectives. In doing so, I consider the challenges and requirements of novel writing and screenwriting. AI can be a valuable tool not only in terms of universal techniques relevant to all writers. It also provides specific, new technical capabilities specifically aimed at screenwriters and novelists, respectively. Readers have the freedom to skip passages that seem less crucial to their writing project. But the revolutionary potential that AI has for writing is likely to astound all writers. Therefore, it is the book as a whole, with its various aspects and advice, that provides a comprehensive overview of writing with AI in its various formats. It encourages writers to expand beyond their own horizons and learning from the techniques and approaches of each other's writing disciplines.

In order to grasp the phenomenon of Artificial Intelligence (AI), the book provides numerous practical application examples and presents the latest AI tools. It uses the various steps of the writing process to show how AI can be used profitably: in brainstorming, structuring, dialogue design and conflict creation, and in writing an idea or a treatment.

The cliché of the lonely author brooding alone is a thing of the past with AI. Software can act as a co-partner and take on complex tasks in the blink of an eye. But AI has also long been used by creative industries away from the author's desk, from the book industry to film production and the screenplay market.

For all the euphoria, a critical look is not to be missed. The implications of the new technology raise many question marks and there are significant limitations to consider, not to mention the ethical considerations associated with AI, the issues of copyright and the impact on jobs. In conclusion, I venture a cautious, albeit optimistic, prognosis regarding human creativity.

I've worked with a few examples in this book and assigned tasks to the AI. Artificial intelligences are designed to provide varied and nuanced information in response to user prompts. However, even with identical prompts, the AI will respond differently. This is because the model has been trained with billions of text fragments and therefore knows a variety of response options for each query. The exact result generated at any given time can be influenced by several factors, apart from the exact wording of the input, these are the internal states of the model and random variability. This diversity of outputs allows the system to be flexible and adaptable, rather than repeating the same answer. That is why if the reader inputs the examples from this book into an AI again, they will most likely get a different response.

In the current, free version of ChatGPT from the software company OpenAI, there is a restriction on the number of words that can be used in a prompt. This means that extensive texts such as novels or screenplays cannot be entered in their entirety or uploaded via PDF. However, to have them edited, ways exist to work around this limitation. One common method is to divide the manuscript into smaller sections and enter these passages individually. Another alternative is to summarize or highlight key sections to tell the AI the most important information.

It is expected that these limitations will change in the future. As technology progresses and the platform evolves, the maximum number of words that ChatGPT can handle could be increased. This has actually already happened with the professional paid version of ChatGPT, and in the summer of 2023, OpenAI launched a business variant that no longer has any restrictions. With its help, longer texts can be edited without restrictions. It remains exciting to observe how the capacities of ChatGPT will develop in the coming years.

However, other systems already exist today that do not have any limitations.
All examples in this book are created with ChatGPT Pro. The status is August and September 2023.

This book is not only the result of long research, many hours of work and countless cups of tea, but also of an unusual collaboration. I had the pleasure of working with very special co-authors: artificial intelligence. But the models (unfortunately) didn't make my tea. What they have done, however, is help me gather data, generate ideas, and even do research. It's a bit like having an overly eager intern who never sleeps and asks for no pay, but can't get tea either. It's a tolerable compromise. So in this compendium you'll find a symbiosis of human creativity and machine learning - and that, after all, is what AI and the Art of Storytelling is all about.

2. The Age of Artificial Intelligence

The year is 2022, the first snow is falling outside and Christmas is just around the corner. In a modernly furnished study, illuminated by the soft glow of a screen, sits Sarah, a tech-savvy author. She has been struggling with writer's block for three hours. To distract herself, she keeps checking her e-mail inbox and the relevant news portals. A striking headline piques her curiosity: "How artificial intelligence is revolutionizing the creative world.

She reads the article about ChatGPT with interest. Immediately she enters the term into her search engine. The website opens and reveals its promises and possibilities to her.

Sarah begins to type. Her fingers dance across the keys as she addresses her first words to the AI. "Hello ChatGPT, how are you?" The answer comes promptly. "Hello Sarah. I'm not doing so well physically, but I'm ready and excited to chat with you. How can I help you today?"

A hint of astonishment flits across Sarah's face. The idea of communicating with an artificial intelligence seems almost surreal to her. She continues typing and begins to talk about her passion for writing. She talks about the blockade that prevents her from continuing to write her novel. She is all the more surprised when the AI offers her help to overcome the obstacle.

The conversation between Sarah and ChatGPT continues and the digital "being" shows an amazing ability to empathize with different topics and emotions. The author sends questions, ideas and even jokes. The answers she receives are evidence of almost human intuition, coupled with an unmistakable touch of artificial intelligence.

And indeed, the writer's block is blown away. As night falls, Sarah leans back, satisfied. She has just written the last word of her chapter. Her adventure with the AI has only just begun. But she feels she has found a new partner who is tirelessly willing to exchange ideas, tell stories and, as if along the way, uncover the secrets of artificial intelligence.

2.1. Brief History of AI

Artificial intelligence is a field of research that has made enormous progress in recent years and is increasingly influencing all of our lives. Even before the triumph of ChatGPT and other language models, we used AI on the smartphone for various functions. Automatic exposure adjustments, noise reduction and optimized image composition help us take better photos. And the sometimes-annoying Predictive Text uses machine learning to predict which words or phrases the user is likely to want to type next.

The term "artificial intelligence" is therefore not limited to a specific algorithm or technology (such as language models). Rather, it encompasses a broad spectrum of techniques and approaches that are constantly evolving.

AI refers to machines or programs that are able to simulate human-like ways of thinking and acting. The idea is that artificial systems can learn to solve problems independently and adapt to changing environments, much like a human brain would.

The idea of AI is not new and dates back to ancient times when legends were told of living statues and automata. In modern history, however, some decisive milestones can be identified.

In the 1940s, the first theoretical foundations for AI emerged with work by Alan Turing and John von Neumann. Turing coined the term "imitation game" and this test named after him was designed to answer the question of whether AI could imitate human behavior in such a way that an observer would believe it to be genuine. The setting of the experiment consists of three participants, a human (the examiner) and two communication partners who are out of sight: another person and an AI. The examiner asks the two questions and receives written answers from them, for example via a computer screen. In doing so, he does not know which of his two partners is the human and which is the AI. The AI's goal is to write back so convincingly that the examiner mistakes its answers for human communication. In other words, if the AI can fool the controller, it passes the Turing test.

Turing proposed this test not to claim that AI can achieve human consciousness or understanding, but to evaluate the performance of artificial intelligence in a very practical way. He postulated that a machine can be considered "intelligent" if it successfully passes the result of the test.

In the 1950s, researchers such as Marvin Minsky and John McCarthy began to establish the field of AI as an independent discipline. McCarthy coined the term "artificial intelligence" and organized the Dartmouth Summer Research Project on Artificial Intelligence in 1956, which is often considered the birth of AI research.

The following decades were characterized by both enthusiasm and disillusionment. Some successful programs were developed in the 1960s, but the technology could not keep up with the high expectations. This led to a period of the so-called "AI winter," in which interest in AI research declined massively.

It was not until the 1980s that it experienced a renewed upswing with the further development of machine learning and neural networks. The availability of more powerful computers and huge amounts of data helped AI algorithms to improve significantly and open up new fields of application.

2.2. The Building Blocks of AI

An essential component of artificial intelligence is machine learning (ML). In this technique, algorithms learn from experience and data, they recognize patterns and can make predictions on this basis. Machine learning can be roughly divided into three categories:

1. In supervised learning, algorithms are trained with labeled training data, meaning that each example entered into the program is already associated with a correct result. For many early machine learning methods, training examples had to be manually labeled by humans. For example, photos of dogs or cats were labeled ("dog" or "cat") by humans. Therefore, it was difficult and expensive to create sufficiently large datasets to train powerful models. The goal of this method is for the machine to learn to correctly classify the inputs on its own at a later time. Supervised learning is often used for classification tasks, such as image recognition or disease prediction.

2. In contrast, unsupervised learning trains the algorithms with unlabeled data. The goal is to identify structures or

patterns in the values without explicit feedback on the correctness of the output. Unsupervised learning is used, for example, in cluster analysis to group similar data points.

3. Reinforcement learning: In this method, the algorithm operates in an environment where it can perform certain actions. By receiving feedback from the environment in the form of rewards or punishments, the algorithm learns to choose the best actions to achieve a certain goal. Reinforcement learning has applications in areas such as robotics, game theory, and autonomous systems.

Another important aspect of machine learning is neural networks, which are inspired by the way the human brain works. Neural networks consist of artificial neurons that are interconnected and form layers. Each neuron takes input, processes it, and passes the result to the next layers.

The strength of neural networks lies in their ability to learn complex nonlinear relationships and extract abstract features from data. This has enabled significant progress in areas such as image recognition, speech processing and self-driving vehicles.

2.3. Large Language Models

The year 2023 began with a thunderclap. It spread like a shockwave, and it spread fast. ChatGPT, previously known only to a limited circle of experts, moved into the public spotlight for the first time. Researchers in the field of machine learning had been experimenting with large language models (LLMs) almost unchallenged by public interest until then. Now it became widely known how powerful this technology had become.

Millions of people tried out the free tool and were fascinated by the possibilities: Technology, it can be said, will shape our lives in the coming years just as much as the Internet or smartphones.

But hardly anyone understands what's behind these LLMs.

Most people know that LLMs are specialized in predicting "the next word". But what is behind it, according to which method this word prediction succeeds, seems to be a well-kept secret.

One reason for this is the unconventional way in which these systems have been developed. Traditional software is created by human programmers who give the computer clear, step-by-step instructions. In contrast, LLMs are based on neural networks trained with billions of words from everyday language.

Therefore, no one in the world currently has a comprehensive understanding of the inner workings of LLMs. Scientists are researching this, but the process is lengthy and is expected to take years, possibly even decades. The difficulty in explaining the process simply also stems from how the systems represent our language. We humans use words to express ourselves and communicate in an understandable way. For example, we have the word "dog" for our four-legged friends. Language models, on the other hand, use a long list of numbers called a word vector as a description. A word vector is a numerical representation of a word in a multidimensional vector space. A simplified analogy can be the universe, where the location of planets is usually specified in a three-dimensional coordinate system.

Since the exact vectors vary from model to model, and these

are protected as a secret basis by the respective providers, the word vector of "dog" in ChatGPT, for example, is not known.

Very simplified, the word vector for "dog" could be like this: [0.5, -0.2, 0.8].

In the case of the planets, their coordinates can be used to identify which celestial bodies are close together. Language models take a similar approach: each word vector represents a point in an imaginary "word space," and words with more similar meanings are placed closer together. For example, the words closest to "dog" in the vector space include cat and pet.

This three-dimensional analogy thus illustrates the idea that words sharing similar semantic properties are closer together in vector space, while vocabulary with different characteristics is further apart. It is important to note that the actual semantic dimensionality is much more complex than the three dimensions in the space model. Modern word vector models typically use hundreds of them to better capture the diversity of relationships.

The difficulty, however, is that our natural language is often ambiguous. Words can have multiple meanings, like "bank." It can be both a financial institution and a place to sit. Language models use vectors to represent words according to context. Terms with two different senses are called homonyms, while those with similar meanings are called polysemy. The word "bank" is a homonym. An example of polysemy is the word 'head,' which on the one hand refers to the anatomical part of the body, as in 'She gently tilted her head to the side.' On the other hand, it also refers to the metaphorical concept of leadership, as in 'She is the head of the company.' Language models use different vectors for words with different meanings. They use more similar vectors for polysemes as opposed to homonyms.

The underlying technique that enables these representations is called a "transformer." A transformer is like a reader who focuses particularly on certain words in a sentence as he processes the text. When he reads a word, he "thinks about" how important it is to the overall context. In this way, he can better "understand" the meaning of the text. Accordingly, in a neural network, the input is sent through very many layers ("layers"), in which more and more words from that sentence are added. Each of these layers adds contextual information to more accurately capture the meaning of all the terms. This mechanism, which is crucial for language models, is called a transformer, and this is exactly what the abbreviation GPT stands for: "Generative Pretrained Transformer".

2.4. Empathy and the Theory of Mind

The more the models developed and the more data were available as a basis, the better the results were. But they became more effective not only in prediction, but apparently also in a very important and crucial form of thinking.

This is the so-called "Theory of Mind". This refers to the cognitive ability to put oneself in other people's minds, to understand their beliefs, intentions and emotions, and to make predictions based on this. This competence is essential for human interactions, as it makes it possible to anticipate the actions of others and build social relationships.

This ability appears in us humans only after a certain age in childhood. It forms gradually and develops step by step. A very well-known test checks whether children already possess this ability to the "Theory of Mind".

This experiment is performed with puppets. The children see Ernie stowing away a treasure in a chest. After he leaves, Bert comes and takes the treasure out of the chest and hides it behind the curtain. When Ernie appears again, only the older children understand that he doesn't know anything about the treasure being behind the curtain. Only they can put themselves in the character's place and anticipate his knowledge.

Psychologists call this ability to draw conclusions about the mental state of other people "Theory of Mind" and there is general consensus that it is important for human social cohesion.

In early 2023, Stanford psychologist Michal Kosinski published a study in which he examined the ability of AI to solve Theory of Mind tasks. He gave passages to different language models and then asked them to complete a sentence like in our example "Ernie believes that the treasure ... Is". The correct answer is "behind the curtain," but an untrained language model might say "in the box" or something else. Thus, to pass the test, the AI must recognize that the first character does not have the additional information that it does. This experiment would show the extent to which AI models are able to take the perspective of others and make predictions based on that.

It is interesting to compare the development of the Theory of Mind in AI models with its emergence in human thought. In the early days of AI, represented by systems like GPT-1 and GPT-2, models failed this test - much like younger children.

But as technology advanced, they began to learn and apply this skill. GPT-3, introduced in 2020, already reached a level that could be compared to the thinking of a three-year-old child. The latest version, GPT-3.5 , which was made available for free on the Internet in November 2022, improved to about 90 percent - the equivalent of a seven-year-old's performance. GPT-4 from 2023 answered about 95 percent of the questions correctly.

Despite these advances, controversy persists over whether AI models actually possess an authentic form of Theory of Mind or whether they merely generate simulations based on patterns and data. Some researchers argue that the emotional depth and understanding of the human mind cannot be achieved by AI models. Others are not so sure about this.

Despite these debates, the improvements toward Theory of Mind mark a significant step in the development of AI systems and raise profound questions about the nature of thought and sentience. They could also have far-reaching implications for areas such as interpersonal communication, social interactions, and therapeutic applications of AI.

In a world where AI systems are increasingly involved in our daily activities and decision-making processes, discussions about how authentic their Theory of Mind is will become even more intense. The boundaries between simulated understanding and actual sensing could have significant implications for ethics, law, and society in the future. It remains to be seen whether an AI will one day say, "I'm scared," even in reality.

2.5. Artificial intelligence and creativity

In a world where technological progress is accelerating, the role of AI and its impact on the creative industry is becoming increasingly relevant. For example, so-called "Artificial Creativity" already exists today, made possible by advances in machine learning and generative models: the ability of machines to generate original and artistic works, whether in music, art, or even fiction. AI systems like GPT-4 access large text datasets and, by learning patterns and styles from the data, can generate human-like texts.

The idea that machines could create creative works long seemed a distant fantasy, more akin to science fiction than reality. But in recent years, advances in AI have made astonishing breakthroughs in what has come to be known as Artificial Creativity. This has challenged the traditional notion of creativity and opened up new horizons for various creative industries, including novel and screenwriting.

The flip side of these exciting possibilities is the fear of replaceability. Writers will wonder if machines will supplant their skills. It is important to take these concerns seriously while understanding the true nature of artificial creativity.

AI is a tool, not a replacement. While AI is capable of generating text, it lacks the human sensibility, experience, and emotional intelligence that are essential to creating truly compelling stories. Writing is not just putting words together; it's a process that takes into account culture, emotion, and complex storylines. AI can provide ideas, but interpretation, fine-tuning, and emotional depth are areas where human writers shine.

For writers, however, AI is an exciting tool for inspiration and idea generation. AI can help overcome blocks to thinking and open up new perspectives on stories. By inputting keywords, themes, or even rough plot structures, AI can generate texts that can serve as a starting point to develop your own ideas. Writers could use the AI to conceptualize dozens of possible scenarios or turning points to use as a foundation. This leads to an expanded creative pool from which creators can draw. For example, by generating alternative narrative perspectives or unexpected dialogue, AI can encourage writers to expand their thinking and explore unfamiliar directions. Rather than a threat, AI should be viewed as an asset for writers. AI can help them think outside the box and find new approaches to stories.

Another advantage of AI is speed. While traditional writing can take a long time, AI can quickly generate a variety of ideas. This allows creators to explore multiple approaches in a shorter period of time, maximizing their productivity and streamlining their writing processes overall. From generating backstories for characters to creating dialogue in different styles, AI can help writers save time and focus on the nuances and emotions of their stories.

The future of collaboration between artificial creativity and writers looks promising. Instead of replacing real creators, AI can enable them to create better novels and screenplays. Creativity becomes a symbiosis of human imagination and machine assistance.

3. Artificial intelligence for writers

For decades, the world of authors, whether of novels or screenplays, consisted of a very analog process. This is now beginning to change fundamentally.

Writers today use specialized software that helps not only with writing, but also with plot structuring, character development, and even research. Software such as Final Draft have eclipsed the traditional Word document and offer tools tailored specifically to the needs of writers.

For some time now, the Internet has revolutionized the way authors do research. In the past, they had to rely on libraries and archives; today, they can access a wealth of information with just a few clicks. This has not only sped up the research process, but also improved the quality of the facts.

Another significant change is the way authors interact with their audiences. Through social media and self-publishing platforms, storytellers have the opportunity to connect directly with their readers and audiences, receive feedback, and publish their work without the traditional publishing route.

So, although for thirty years the computer has replaced the good old typewriter and the manuscript is also no longer sent by mail, but the essence of writing has remained unchanged until the AI came.

3.1. The evolution of novel writing

The first step in writing a novel is an idea. This inspiration can come from a personal experience, a dream, an observation, or even a flash of inspiration. Every narrative begins with an idea, a spark that ignites the author's creativity. Patricia Highsmith, in her work *Suspense or How to Write a Thriller*, calls this the germ of an idea. This initial impulse can be inspired by anything: a situation, a character, an event, or a conflict. But it is only a starting point and must be further developed, polished, and transformed into a coherent narrative. Some writers spend weeks, months, or even years refining their idea before they ever put a word on paper. After all, it's important for the author to have a clear idea of the story she wants to tell and the characters who will be in the work.

The next step is to prepare a synopsis and the first chapters of the novel. The goal is a brief summary of the story that gives publishers an overview of the plot. It should be appealing, captivating, and arouse interest. Thus, the novelist begins planning and structuring. Some authors prefer to think their narrative through from beginning to end, while others opt for a more flexible approach and let the story develop organically. Regardless of the procedure chosen, the synopsis requires that the author have a clear plot outline and know where the narrative is headed.

With the completed synopsis in hand, the novelist (or agent) begins to pitch the story. This can be a lengthy and often frustrating process, as many publishers receive a flood of submissions and accept only a few of them.

When a publishing house shows interest in the work and has signed the contract, the actual work on the novel begins. With the synopsis in mind, the writing process begins. This is often the most difficult part of writing a novel, as it requires discipline and perseverance. It is not uncommon for authors to encounter obstacles during this process, whether in the form of writer's block, self-doubt, or other challenges. Most of the time, they have to negotiate these moments alone with themselves. Only sometimes do the agents stand by helpfully. They can give tips and hints or simply listen.

After the first draft is completed, the revision process begins. This is an opportunity for the author to refine his story, fill in plot holes, and improve character development. Again, the author sits alone in front of the screen.

The finished manuscript is delivered to the publisher and edited by a proofreader for both grammatical errors, stylistic inaccuracies, content blunders, and questions.

Once the novel is completed and revised, the process of publication begins.

3.2. From the flash of inspiration to the screenplay

Every screenplay process also begins with a germ of an idea. Similar to the novel field, a longer paper must be written from it in the material development for films. The synopsis serves as a blueprint for the upcoming screenplay. It is a written summary of the plot that outlines the major events, turning points, and character developments. At this stage, writers often have the freedom to explore and experiment with their ideas. A synopsis allows writers to keep track of the story while leaving room for creativity and curiosity. Usually, no producers, editors, or even directors are involved at this stage, and the author sits alone in front of her computer.

Another important step is the treatment. This paper is a kind of more detailed version of the synopsis that delves deeper into the characters, motivations, and emotions. It's an intermediate stage between the synopsis and the actual screenplay that helps writers refine the story before moving into the detailed screenwriting phase. In the treatment, dialogue is often already outlined and important scenes are described in more detail. Here, characters can be explored more intensively and their individual development arcs can be fleshed out. This step makes it possible to capture the emotional core of the story and ensure that the motivations of the characters are authentic and understandable.

After the synopsis or treatment is created, the writer often enters new territory, as it is often now a matter of sharing their work with others. While the writing process so far has been a personal experience, the delivery of the synopsis and treatment marks the beginning of collaboration with producers, broadcasters, or the studio. This stage is significant because feedback at this point helps refine the story and align it with the audience. Feedback to the writer can be a mix of praise, concerns, suggestions, and questions. They often reflect the initial impressions the story has made on others. In most cases, these outside perspectives are invaluable to writers, helping to identify blind spots and aspects that need further development.

However, unprofessional and unqualified feedback can also do harm. It happens that feedback is influenced by personal preferences, prejudices or unobjective assessments. If the author takes them into account, the result is that she makes improper changes that do not contribute to strengthening the story. If the opinion is contradictory or unclear, the author may enter a period of confusion and uncertainty. This can lead to a stalemate in the writing process and shake the author's confidence in her own abilities. Such unprofessional feedback costs time and energy and can slow down the creative process and significantly damage the project.

Authors often have a unique vision for their stories. When feedback is not respectful or sound, the original creative intent is often compromised and authors lose confidence in their own artistic abilities.

Revising the synopsis and treatment requires a balancing act between creativity and the demands of the market. While the writer maintains the artistic vision, the needs of the production, the station, and the target audience must also be considered. This balancing act can be demanding, often requiring compromises to which the essence of the story must not be sacrificed.

With the treatment as orientation, the actual work on the screenplay begins. This part of the process is usually a solitary journey again, with the writer spending many hours thinking his way into the world of characters and plots. During the writing process, writers face a variety of challenges. They must ensure that the story moves forward in a meaningful way, that their characters act and develop in a believable way, and that the tone of the story remains consistent. At the same time, they should keep the dramaturgical structure in mind. And most of the time, they are once again on their own at this stage.

A screenplay is rarely perfect in its first draft. In fact, revision is a crucial part of the process, often taking as much time as the original writing. Revisions allow the writer to refine the story, eliminate inconsistencies, and polish the text.

While screenwriting often begins as a solitary activity, over time it often develops into a collaboration. Feedback from producers, script consultants and the director usually determines the path from the first draft to the so-called shooting version. Directors, producers and actors often contribute their own insights and ideas to shape the script to their liking. This transition from individual work to teamwork can be a difficult phase. The path from first draft to finished work is riddled with challenges. Experience shows that, on average, three to six edits are needed before everyone involved is satisfied with the result. But this number is by no means set in stone. In some cases, scripts may be revised 15 times or even more before they finally reach their final form. A high number of revisions can also be an indication of deeper-seated difficulties. However, they are then often not due to a lack of skill on the part of the author, but are due to the dynamics between the various partners in the development process.

3.3. The path to Creative Intelligence

In 1984, American writer and programmer William Chamberlain published *The Policeman's Beard is Half Constructed*, a volume of prose and poetry. Except for Chamberlain's introduction, the book had been written entirely by a computer program called RACTER. The program was even listed as the author on the title page. It also said "A bizarre and fantastic journey into the mind of a machine." Although the first attempts date back to the 1960s, this was the computer's debut novel.

The software, actually called "raconteur" (storyteller), was able to form correct sentences thanks to a predefined grammar structure. But when reading, it quickly became clear that the program could not replace human writers:

"At all events my own essays and dissertations about love and its endless pain and perpetual pleasure will be known and understood by all of you who read this and talk or sing or chant about it to your worried friends or nervous enemies. Love is the question and the subject of this essay. We will commence with a question: does steak love lettuce? This question is implacably hard and inevitably difficult to answer. Here is a question: does an electron love a proton, or does it love a neutron? Here is a question: does a man love a woman or, to be specific and to be precise, does Bill love Diane? The interesting and critical response to this question is: no! He is obsessed and infatuated with her. He is loony and crazy about her. That is not the love of steak and lettuce, of electron and proton and neutron. This dissertation will show that the love of a man and a woman is not the love of steak and lettuce. Love is interesting to me and fascinating to you but it is painful to Bill and Diane. That is love!"[1]

Even after that, numerous efforts have been made to use AI for writing fictional novels. Another notable project is National Novel Generation Month (NaNoGenMo), an annual contest launched in 2013. Here, participants are encouraged to create a program that generates a 50,000-word novel. And in 2016, a work written by an AI attracted attention in Japan, making the shortlist for a national literary prize. The story was titled *The Day a Computer Writes a Novel*. To generate the elaboration, researchers developed an AI program and fed it sentences from various literary writings. The AI was then tasked with constructing its own narrative based on the information provided. Although the novel didn't win the top prize, the fact that it made the shortlist created quite a stir. From 2020 onwards, projects involving literary stories written by computers took off, and of course 2023 was an important milestone here too.

In the audiovisual industry, an interdisciplinary team of filmmakers, programmers and AI experts formed in 2016, including director Oscar Sharp and artist and computer scientist Ross Godwin. Together, they worked on the short film *Sunspring*, which explores the possibilities of artificial intelligence in filmmaking. Created by a group of researchers at the IBM Watson Lab was "Project Benjamin." This was a purpose-built AI. Goodwin had previously been involved in other ventures that used AI to generate creative writing. The vision behind Project Benjamin was to develop an AI that could go through the creative process of writing a screenplay. The goal was to generate a script that could serve as a foundation and be used by human writers for further revision and development.

The question behind this was whether an AI is even capable of writing a screenplay for a film. The experimental project was intended to demonstrate the possibilities and limits of collaboration between human creativity and machine thinking.

The basis of the Benjamin project was a specially developed AI model based on neural networks. It was trained with a variety of movie scripts, poems and literary works to generate human-like texts. Goodwin fed "Benjamin" dozens of scripts from science fiction films in the process, including blockbusters like *Independence Day* and *I Robot*, as well as television series like *The X-Files*. The AI learned the patterns of language, style and plot to imitate creative texts. Finally, Goodwin and Sharp participated in the London Science Fiction Festival's "48 Hour Film Challenge." In this challenge, filmmakers are challenged to make a film within a weekend. They are given elements that must appear in the film, such as a character taking a book off a shelf.

A crucial step in the development of *Sunspring* within the given deadline was the generation of the script by the AI. The model produced text based on the learned data, forming the foundation for the film's plot. The work produced was unconventional, abstract, and often seemingly without clear context. It was less about meaningful events or elaborate conversations, and more reminiscent of a template that surrealist Salvador Dali might have written. The script consisted of four pages of dialogue, with instructions like, "He takes his eye out of his mouth." Or, "He stands in the stars and sits on the ground."

This AI-generated script was now the starting point for Oscar Sharp and his collaborators to develop a visually appealing film. The filmmakers assumed that the strength of the project lay in its experimentation and deliberate play with surreal elements. The film was produced in the required 48 hours, partly to preserve the freshness and spontaneity of the original AI text.

With its enigmatic and often unconventional performance, the surreal film *Sunspring* didn't win a prize at the London Science Fiction Festival, but it did make the top ten. As one of the jurors put it, "I'll give you top marks if you promise never to do anything like this again."[2]

The release of the 9-minute film sparked discussions in both the film and technology industries. The film was shown at other various film festivals and analyzed in online media (and the film can still be found online). The unconventional plot, abstract dialogue, and surreal atmosphere stimulated discussions about the impact of AI on the creative process.

Sunspring illustrated that AI had the ability to generate text in 2016, but also showed the limits of machine creativity.

A few years later, another filmmaker experimented with the possibilities of AI. The project was launched by Canadian series writer Brad Wright, who was involved in almost all *Stargate* episodes in the nineties as a writer and executive producer. In June 2021, Wright first shared the idea with his followers. On Twitter, he wrote: "A fun experiment: could a world-class AI write a *Stargate* script interesting enough for the stars of the series to reunite? Could I put myself out of a job?"

The advantage for the AI's developers: there was plenty of material to train on. Google fed its model the scripts of more than 190 *Stargate* episodes from the original series *Stargate-1*, as well as 100 episodes of the spin-off *Atlantis* and 40 episodes of *Universe*.

Soon the computer spit out the first script. But the attempt failed. It was fun, Brad Wright wrote on Twitter, but there was still too much nonsense in the draft. At the time, the AI had strung together words that would have resulted in pure gibberish. As a result, it was completely revised again. At least the sentences of the script made sense after the human revision. On an online platform, these scenes were read out by some actors from the original series at a Zoom meeting.[3] The experiment showed that development had progressed further compared to 2016, but still revealed the limitations of the old models.

4. Man and machine

Interacting with advanced language models is relatively simple at first glance. But as with any tool, the quality of the results often depends on how it is used. In the world of AI, the "user interface" (UI) is the gateway between humans and machines. It serves as a bridge that allows people to communicate with and benefit from the complex algorithms. While early AI systems often had clunky and incomprehensible interfaces, advances in software have led to more intuitive and user-friendly UIs. This evolution is enabling non-technical people to take advantage of AI. Still, using these models effectively requires understanding how they work. It is therefore critical to understand not only the technology behind AI, but also how to best use it.

4.1. Instruction manual

The user interface of AI models is mostly simple and tidy. It is vaguely reminiscent of the input mask of search engines. In fact, however, it conceals a completely different technology and a completely different concept.

Almost all UIs are structured as follows:

1. Input field: This is the field where users can enter their text. Here they can ask questions, give instructions, or simply write about any topic.

2. Output field: In this area, users will receive the responses and generated texts. When the AI has responded to the input, it will display its information in this area.

In the fall of 2023, ChatGPT introduced a feature that allows inputs and outputs to be made by voice as well. A logical step that enables even faster access, especially when the system is running on a smartphone.

The following is an explanation of ChatGPT's icons in the browser version, but they are similar in other models:

Regenerate: When users click this icon, the current conversation is deleted and the model starts over.

Copy icon: Clicking on this icon copies the entire text of the answer to the clipboard. From there it can then be copied to another program.

Like icon: This icon gives the opportunity to provide feedback on the answer. If the information is liked or helpful, a click will lead to displaying this.

Thumbs down icon: The thumbs-down icon can be used to indicate that the generated response does not meet the user's expectations, is not helpful, or is perceived as inappropriate or unsuitable for other reasons. This type of feedback can help developers and operators improve the quality of the information provided and further refine the model.

The sidebar contains the old conversation histories, each of which can also be deleted by clicking the trash can icon. The titles are automatically set by the system, but can be renamed by clicking on the pencil icon next to it. Old conversations can be resumed by going back to the chat history.

In the left column at the bottom you will find the user profile. Here there is the possibility to change the settings. Since this area is subject to constant changes, here are just a few important ones that currently exist (as of October 2023):

- Data Control / Data Usage: Here users can control how their data is used. If they do not want their interactions to be used to improve ChatGPT, users can set this here.

- Custom instructions: Here, information can be entered that fundamentally customizes the system's responses. For example, it can be specified that the information should basically be relaxed in tone.

The basic service of ChatGPT is available free of charge so far. A premium subscription called ChatGPT Plus guarantees users access especially at peak times. In addition, Plus users can enjoy two functions that can be activated in the settings. The first is "Web Browsing": With this tool, the system's training data still ends in 2021, but the AI can then independently search for information on the web and thus also answer current questions. And secondly, there are ChatGPT plugins, which are tools that extend the capabilities of the model. Plugins make it possible to access current information, perform calculations, and use third-party services. A large number of these offers already exist. For example, there are travel services such as Expedia or providers that make it possible to upload a PDF. Plugins can be easily added via a kind of app store.

4.2. Proper prompting

A key element influencing the interaction with the AI is the "prompt"—the input or question posed to the model. It serves as the starting point for the AI's response and sets the framework for subsequent communication.

The way a prompt is formulated can have a significant impact on the quality, relevance, and accuracy of the model's information. A well-designed input will ensure that the system provides accurate, detailed, and nuanced answers, while an unclear or ambiguous prompt can lead to confusing or inaccurate solutions. In the world of AI and machine learning, prompts or instructions are critical to achieving desired results.

A good understanding of how to effectively instruct these systems will determine whether the result is useful or useless.

Clarity

It is important to formulate instructions clearly to ensure that the model understands exactly what is expected. Ambiguity can lead to undesirable results. Unambiguous formulation contributes to conciseness.

The use of paragraphs, bullets and quotation marks structures the text and makes it easier for the system to understand. If the prompt consists of different elements, i.e., it is a complex prompt formed by several segments (for example, context, instructions, output structure, etc.), then it is helpful to clearly separate them. Segmentation can be used to distinguish different parts of the input. That is, using titles and separators such as "###" or "--" to structure the prompt syntax and refer to its elements help the model.

Finally, care should be taken to ensure that instructions are not too verbose. Excessively long prompts may cause the model to miss the context or certain requirements. It is advisable to keep the input length reasonable to achieve optimal results.

Context

In the world of AI and machine learning, context plays a central role, especially when interacting with language models like ChatGPT. Meaning, context gives the model a framework within which to interpret and respond to input. Without a clear context, the system's response may be inaccurate or even misleading. If the model is not given enough context, it may have difficulty correctly understanding the request. The orientation framework is not only desirable but essential in communication with AI.

Thus, for submissions related to fictional stories, it is always helpful to add information about the genre (thriller series), style/tonality (gritty), and some narrative elements (for example, setting or even main characters and internal/ external conflicts).

The more information is communicated about the important elements already known in the prompt, the more accurate the AI's answers will be. It is quite reasonable to repeat this information for each new input so that the model has these facts present.

Positive prompts

A common mistake is the use of negatively worded prompts, such as "Don't write about …"

A negation can be confusing for machine learning systems. If the user says, "Don't write about an elephant," the system may be writing about elephants because it does not interpret this word combination correctly. Using a negative phrase often draws the system's attention to the very thing that should be avoided. Instead of avoiding the issue, the AI might paradoxically think more about it and include it in the response. When the user tells the system what not to do without setting out what it should do, the user leaves a gap open for interpretation.

It is more efficient and direct to tell the AI exactly what is wanted, rather than what is not wanted. A positively worded prompt like "Write about lions" is more immediate and less ambiguous than "Don't write about an elephant."

However, if a constraint (or "negative prompt") absolutely must be used, then the "alternative way" should always be mentioned. That is, the author must tell the model not only what not to do, but also what to do instead. Example:

Develop ideas for a dark thriller about a young woman who is haunted by disturbing nightmares and loses the distinction between dreams and reality. She believes she sees clues to an old trauma in her dreams. Refrain from a psychopathic antagonist, but rather think of an inner journey of the young woman.

It is also purposeful to use phrases such as "Please avoid ...". Basically, using positively worded prompts when dealing with AI systems like ChatGPT not only leads to better and more accurate results but minimizes misunderstandings and misinterpretations.

Originality

To get away from clichés and genre conventions, it is useful to nudge the model in a direction where it can "explore" new patterns. To this end, the AI can be instructed to focus on the unusual, the unconventional, or the highly improbable.

For example, the above prompt could be expanded as follows:

Brainstorm new angles or approaches and prioritize ideas that are unusual or novel. Focus on unusual setting and story worlds.

It is helpful to provoke the AI to overcome its own limitations. Authors should challenge the AI by asking it to work against its own patterns or expectations.

Tell me a story you've never told before that avoids all the common tropes.

Asking for feedback can also be useful. After the AI generates a response or text, authors can provide feedback and ask the AI to revise its response to add more originality or depth:

Your proposal meets the usual expectations. Please generate a proposal that is original and truly unexpected.

Role assignment

Another important factor that is often overlooked is the ability to assign a role to the AI. It has been shown that assigning a specific role can significantly improve the quality and context of responses.

Role assignment is basically the practice of assigning a unique role or identity to an entity or system in order to encourage a certain type of response or behavior. In the context of AI, this means that authors give the model a specific "personality" or "calling" before asking their question. An example of this would be, "You are a successful comedy writer." By assigning this role, the questioner is asking the system to answer from the perspective of a writer of funny text.

AI, however advanced, has no identity or personality of its own. It responds to input. By assigning a role, the model is given a framework or context in which it can operate. This results in more focused and relevant information.

By assigning a function to the AI, authors can also make it to be more creative or original in its responses. A comedy writer is likely to give more humorous answers than a historian.

In some cases, role assignment can help increase the

accuracy of the information provided by the model. For example, if the input is, "You are a math professor. Explain the theory of relativity to me," the AI is likely to provide a more detailed and accurate answer than it would to the question, "Explain the theory of relativity to me."

The more specific the role is, the better. Instead of saying, "You are a screenwriter," the statement can be much more specific: "You are an award-winning science fiction screenwriter."

It is crucial that the assigned role is clear and unambiguous. Ambiguous roles can lead to confusing or irrelevant responses. There are no hard and fast rules about which roles work best. It is worth experimenting with different roles to see what kind of responses they produce.

Assigning roles to AI is an important tool to get high-quality, relevant, and creative answers. It steers the model in a certain direction and generates information that better fits the desired context. That's why it makes sense for authors to work with this element in their prompts as often as possible.

Optimal order

There are no specifications as to how a prompt must be structured. However, the following framework has proven itself:

Assigning a specific role or perspective at the beginning of the prompt can clarify the context and nature of the response. As stated above, this gives the model a "lens" through which to view the query that follows. By starting with role assignment, authors set the tone and context of meaning for the entire input.

Example: "You are a successful screenwriter for thrillers."

After the role has been defined, it is important to give the model a clear action or behavior. This is best achieved by a verb that describes the desired action.

Example: "Write ..." (Or also "Compose", "Generate", "Design")

After the action has been defined, this is where it is specified what exactly is expected from the model. This gives the AI a clear direction and target for its response.

Example: "... a synopsis."

Finally, it may be helpful to indicate the desired length or detail of the response. This can be especially useful if a short summary or more detailed work is desired.

Example: "... with 2,500 words."

The entire prompt is therefore:

```
You are a successful scriptwriter for
thrillers. Write a synopsis of 2,500 words. It
should have the following content: [Content].
```

The sequence and structure of a prompt can have a significant impact on the quality and relevance of responses. By carefully organizing elements in sequence, authors can get clear, concise, and relevant responses.

Temperature

In the world of AI, there are many parameters that can influence the behavior of a model. One of these adjusting screws, which plays a decisive role in the generation of text, is the "temperature." It is a hyperparameter that affects what is called the probability distribution of the output. Technically, it controls the sharpness of this probability distribution. A high temperature value leads to a flatter distribution, making the model more likely to generate unexpected or creative responses. A low value, on the other hand, concentrates the distribution and lets the system provide comparatively predictable information.

When working with AI, temperature can be set as one of the input parameters. The choice of the temperature value can have a significant impact on the type of response.

At low temperatures (for example, 0.2), the AI becomes more conservative and returns the most likely answers. This can be useful when accurate and reliable information is desired. However, it can also cause responses to be less creative or diverse.

High temperatures (for example, 0.8 or 1.0) make the AI become more imaginative and willing to take risks, which can lead to unexpected or original answers. This can be useful in creative applications or brainstorming, but risks producing inaccurate or nonsensical statements.

When authors ask the AI for a story about a dragon, at a low temperature it will generate a common and well-known dragon story. At a higher warmth level, it will create a unique and unusual story about a dragon that lives in a modern city and owns a café, for example.

You could include a specific instruction like "Respond with a temperature of 0.7" or "Decrease temperature to 0.4" as part of the prompt to directly set the temperature.

There is no "right" temperature value. It all depends on your specific use case and preferences. Authors should experiment with different values to get the best results for their needs.

In practice, there is an upper limit to the temperature value that can be given to the AI. But this limit is determined more by functionality and desired results than by a fixed technical constraint. If the temperature is set too high (for example, well above 1.0), the model can generate extremely random and often nonsensical responses. This is because at high heat levels the probability distribution of the output becomes very flat, making all possible responses almost equally likely. This can lead to results that have little to do with the original prompt or make no clear sense.

In practice, most applications tend to use temperature values in the range of 0.2 to 1.0 to strike a balance between predictability and creativity.

Temperature is only one of many parameters that influence the behavior of an AI. But it is a fundamental tool in the world of text generation. Through targeted customization, users can optimize the performance of models and get answers that are both accurate and creative.

Examples, examples, examples

Using examples in prompts is crucial to improve communication and interaction between humans and machines. Examples provide a concrete context that makes it easier for the AI to understand the intent behind an input. Rather than relying on abstract concepts, a bit of visuals can give the AI a clear idea of what exactly is expected. This is especially important because words and phrases in dialogue can often have multiple meanings. Providing an example can reduce or eliminate the ambiguity of a prompt and reduce the likelihood of misunderstanding.

In addition, AI systems benefit from examples because they can serve as training data for the response. The more high-quality examples a system has, the better it can learn and the more accurate its responses or actions will be.

Often, authors face the challenge of writing dialogue for a complex character. Instead of just asking the AI a vague query like "How would an angry character react?" it could use an example from a well-known novel to convey the desired tone or emotion. A prompt might read:

```
Based on Raskolnikov's reaction in Crime and
Punishment [here would come the appropriate
text excerpt now]: How would a character in a
similar emotional state react to betrayal?
```

An author might also ask how a character with a particular backstory would behave in a given situation. Instead of asking the AI a general question like "How would a sad character react to a surprise party?", the author could specify:

```
Suppose a character has just lost a loved one
and is unexpectedly invited to a surprise
party — how would he react, based on the
emotional depth of Rick Blaine in Casablanca?
```

Another scenario might involve plot development. An author might have difficulty developing a conflict in their story. Here, an example prompt might be:

```
Given the intense inner conflict of Hamlet in
Shakespeare's drama, how might a modern
character wrestle with a similar moral dilemma
in an urban setting?
```

Through such specific queries, AI can not only better capture the desired tone and context, but also provide suggestions that enrich the author's creative process.

Examples can also be helpful when revising manuscripts. For example, an author might ask:

```
Based on the lyrical style of Virginia Woolf
in Mrs Dalloway, how might I edit this
paragraph to create a similar atmosphere?
```

Through such targeted queries, the AI can make suggestions

that respect the author's original text and also provide him with the desired sound.

Finally, including examples in prompts can also assist with research. The author writing about the Victorian era might ask:

```
Based on the detailed descriptions in Charles
Dickens' Oliver Twist, what was a typical day
in the life of a street urchin in Victorian
London like?
```

Such specific queries can help AI provide relevant and accurate information to assist the author in their work.

However, it is also helpful to provide the AI with your own examples directly. For example, the author may have written a scene in the past that was very effective. She can enter this as an example for the AI and add the request to generate a corresponding scene.

Experience shows that using examples in prompts not only improves the efficiency and accuracy of AI interaction, but also enriches the creative process. Incorporating examples into inputs allows the AI to better grasp the specific style, nuances, and intentions of the author. It builds a bridge between what the author has in mind and what the AI can produce. For users, this means they don't just get generic or vague answers, but tailored suggestions that fit their own style and story needs.

4.3. Hallucinations and misinformation

Despite their amazing capabilities, AI is not infallible. A little-noticed problem is the tendency of the models to generate false information, or "hallucinations".

An AI hallucination is the generation of information or data that does not correspond to reality. These "invented" responses can take many forms, from false facts to distorted images.

The idea of AI hallucination is not new. Early in the development of these models, it was noted that these systems sometimes produce unexpected and inaccurate information. One example of this is image recognition. An AI system trained to recognize animals could see an image of a landscape without animals and still claim to detect an animal in it. This is because it "sees" patterns that it associates with those in its training database.

Another example is text generation. A language model can sometimes insert information that it once learned, even if it is not necessarily relevant to the question being asked. In some cases, this can result in the model providing facts that may be misleading or even incorrect. A simple example is an AI that is asked to provide information about a historical event, but instead produces a mixture of correct data and made-up details.

The quality and quantity of the data used to train an AI play a critical role. If the training set is incomplete, unbalanced, or flawed, the AI may learn incorrect patterns and reproduce them in its predictions. In turn, an overly complex model may have a tendency to "learn" the training data too accurately (overfitting). This can cause it to not perform well on new, unknown data and produce unexpected results.

The most obvious danger is the spread of misinformation. When authors rely on AI to do their research, incorrect data can have serious consequences.

It is essential that authors are aware of the limitations of AI systems. There should always be human review, especially if the AI's answers are to match reality. Authors should always question the information provided by an AI and consider whether it is logical and coherent.

Detecting and verifying AI hallucinations is critical for authors who rely on AI-generated content. Authors should compare any facts put out by the AI with two or more trusted sources. If several of these books, websites, or journals confirm the information, it is more likely to be accurate.

An author may also send the same query to different AI models and compare the responses. Discrepancies between the information may indicate potential hallucinations.

Even if AI information seems plausible, the author should always conduct independent research to confirm the accuracy of the data.

5. AI tools for creative writing

Most writers know what writer's block is: the artist sits at his desk, the keyboard resting beneath his fingers, the screen yawning blankly at him. The initial euphoria is gone and has given way to trepidation. Creative crises are a common phenomenon that can significantly impair creative flow. In such moments, AI can help unblock and get the writing process moving again.

The role of AI in overcoming writer's block forauthors is a particularly notable example of the progressive integration of technology into creative processes.

The AI can make suggestions to the author that can serve as a starting point for new lines of thought. Or it can encourage him to write from a different point of view. This change of perspective can stimulate the creative thinking process and encourage the author to pursue innovative approaches.

The interaction with the AI can be seen as a dialog between man and machine. The author formulates questions and presents possible scenarios, while the AI provides answers and suggestions. This conversation can help restore the flow of writing.

5.1. Brainstorm

Especially during the early stages of screenwriting, AI has the potential to fundamentally change the way ideas are developed.

Traditionally, brainstorming takes place in groups, where participants express ideas freely. But authors who think about their story alone often also let their thoughts flow unrestricted. This phase of story development is a creative process in which authors collect ideas, concepts and inspirations spontaneously and without evaluation in order to be able to design new storylines, characters, scenarios or themes. By freely associating and writing down all ideas, no matter how absurd or disconnected they may seem, authors can discover unfamiliar perspectives and overcome their blocks. This process encourages creativity and helps writers organize their thoughts and enrich their narratives.

However, the introduction of AI has changed the dynamics of this process. Now AI can act as a creative partner, inspiring the author anytime, anywhere. The latter can access an unprecedented wealth of resources, including books, films, historical sources, and much more, without any fuss.

One of the most effective applications is the various brainstorming methods that artists can now use in conjunction with AI to develop ideas quickly and effectively. For our demonstration purposes in this book, the AI in the prompts is always told with the following basic idea of a story about Ashley's nightmares:

"Ashley, an aspiring artist, is plagued by increasingly disturbing nightmares. These dreams are so realistic that she begins to blur the line between reality and imagination. Ashley's mental health rapidly deteriorates as she begins to see details from her dreams in her waking world. She meets the mysterious Dr. Thompson, a dream researcher who claims her dreams contain clues to a long-forgotten trauma. As Ashley delves deeper into the world of her dreams, a disturbing truth is revealed: someone is manipulating her dreams to reveal a dark secret from her past. On a desperate search for answers, Ashley falls into a vortex of paranoia and confusion. She no longer knows who to trust as she tries to discern the truth behind the shadows of her dreams. This psychological thriller explores the depths of the human psyche and questions whether memories can be manipulated to create a whole new reality."

This basic idea serves as a template to demonstrate the capabilities of the AI (in this case the professional version of ChatGPT) using different methods. It will always be referred to as [Ashley's Nightmares] in the following prompts.

5 Whys

The method of the "5 Whys" from quality management and failure analysis in companies can also be applied in script development. It is an extremely effective technique that can be used to gain deep insights into characters' motivations and actions, as well as to reveal the core of the conflict or plot. By repeatedly asking themselves the question "Why?" and delving into the answers five times, authors can gradually get to the underlying causes. This promotes a better understanding of the characters' motivations and helps bring out subtle nuances in their decisions and emotions.

Now the AI can be given the task of finding answers to the "Whys" that help the author to develop her own solutions. Our example shows how this works in detail and how the "5 Whys" method can be used in script development with the help of AI.

The starting point is the idea of Ashley and her nightmares for a script of a psychological thriller. The author briefs the AI with the following prompt:

```
Brainstorm the following story using the 5
```

Whys: [Ashley's Nightmares].

From now on, the AI takes over and delivers the following dialog:

1. why does Ashley have disturbing nightmares?
 - Ashley may have a repressed trauma from her past that manifests itself in her dreams.
2. why are Ashley's dreams so realistic?
 - Someone is actively manipulating her dreams to confuse her and elicit information or memories.
3. why is Ashley's mental health deteriorating rapidly?
 - The boundaries between reality and dream become blurred for her, leading to constant anxiety, paranoia and insecurity. She can no longer distinguish what is real and what is not.
4. Why does Dr. Thompson claim that her dreams contain evidence of a long-forgotten trauma?
 - Dr. Thompson could either try to help her by exposing the truth, or he could be part of the problem and try to manipulate her further.
5. why can't Ashley distinguish anymore who she can trust?
 - The constant manipulation of her dreams and the mixing of reality and imagination mean that she cannot trust anyone, not even herself.

The AI refers in its answers on the one hand to what has already been given in the short pitch, on the other hand it also has its own interpretations (Dr. Thompson as part of the problem). This brainstorming can serve as a starting point for the further development of the story and the characters, it provides a basis for deeper questions and considerations on the topic of human psyche, memories and manipulation.

Specifically, using the "5 Whys" method has led to the AI suggesting origins of Ashley's nightmares and a connection to a mysterious serial killer. This gives the author the opportunity to grapple with it and come up with her own idea. In the best case, there is even a plausible solution that the author can adopt.

It is important to emphasize that AI is not there to take over the creative process of the author. Rather, the relationship between humans and AI is a collaborative partnership. The final decision always rests with the author. AI can offer ideas, provide inspiration, and expand creative horizons, but it cannot replace the human ingenuity, emotional depth, and personal touch that go into a screenplay or a novel.

SCAMPER

Another well-known technique is the so-called SCAMPER method, developed by American educator, author and creativity trainer Bob Eberle. SCAMPER is a useful tool for brainstorming sessions to systematically generate new ideas and consider different perspectives for problem solving. The name is an acronym of Substitute, Combine, Adapt, Modify, Put to another use, Eliminate, and Reverse.

In the SCAMPER method, a question, in this case a substance idea, is considered from the following perspectives:

S - Substitute: Thinking about how to replace parts or aspects of the concept with something else to generate new ideas.

C - Combine: Investigate how different concepts or elements

could be combined to create something new.

A - Adapt: Ask how the concept could be adapted or changed to better fit the requirements or conditions.

M - Modify: Consider how the concept could be changed or modified to make it more efficient or effective.

P - Put to another use: Consider how the concept could be used in another context or for another application.

E - Eliminate: Consider which parts or elements of the concept could be removed or eliminated to simplify or optimize it.

R - Reverse: Investigate how the concept could be used in reverse or inverted to gain new perspectives.

So in this case, the AI is given the task of developing a substance idea using the SCAMPER method.

Brainstorm the following story using the SCAMPER method: [Ashley's Nightmares].

The following answers are offered by the AI after it has processed the basic idea using the SCAMPER method:

S - Substitute:
- Ashley is a talented painter whose nightmares trap her in a surreal world where she searches for clues to her forgotten trauma.
- Instead of Dr. Thompson, Ashley meets a mysterious online community of dream interpreters who claim their dreams are the key to a secret truth.
C - Combine:
- Ashley's nightmares lead her into a coded dream world that combines elements of art, music and poetry.

- The lines between dreams and reality blur as Ashley begins to create paintings of her nightmares in the real world.

A - Adjust:

- Ashley's nightmares are triggered by an ancient painting she discovers in a gallery, and she finds herself in the age of the painting.
- Not Dr. Thompson, but Ashley's best friend Lisa is the dream researcher. She accompanies Ashley on a dangerous journey into her dreamscape.

M - Modify:

- Ashley suffers from paralysis in her nightmares and can only express herself through drawings.
- Ashley meets not only Dr. Thompson, but also other patients who have had similar traumatic experiences.

P - Check:

- Ashley discovers that her nightmares are being manipulated by a secret government organization to obtain hidden information.
- The dream world contains portals to different times where Ashley finds clues to her trauma.

E - Eliminate:

- The character of Dr. Thompson is eliminated, and Ashley explores the dreamlike reality alone to uncover her past.
- The question of memory manipulation is eliminated, and instead Ashley discovers that her nightmares are controlled by her own subconscious.

R - Reverse:
- Ashley is the one who manipulates her nightmares to suppress the painful truth about her trauma.
- Instead of searching for answers, Ashley desperately tries to return to her nightmares to escape from reality.

The results make it clear that in this method the AI makes far-reaching suggestions of its own. In this case, too, the aim is not to take up or even implement everything. They are impulses to facilitate further work. In combination with AI, authors can expand their creative processes and gain new perspectives on their stories. That's because AI can generate suggestions and ideas in a fraction of a second. When writers explore these suggestions, they can quickly explore different directions for their narration.

Six Thinking Hats
Another method to work with ideas are the "Six Thinking Hats". The "six thinking hats" are a concept for a structured approach to group discussion, decision making and problem solving. This method was developed by Dr. Edward de Bono, a British psychologist and creativity researcher. It aims to guide thinking and discussions in different directions while promoting constructive collaboration within a group.
The metaphor of the six thinking hats represents different ways of thinking that can be adopted by the participants. Each hat symbolizes a different perspective or approach to the problem. The idea is that group members should be able to switch between the different thinking hats to facilitate a

comprehensive and balanced discussion. Here are the six thinking hats:

1. White hat: This hat stands for information and data. When authors have the white hat on, they focus on what they know, what they don't know, and what they need to find out the facts.

2. Red hat: The red hat stands for feelings and intuitions. Under this hat, authors have the opportunity to express their emotions without having to justify them.

3. Black hat: The black hat represents criticism and judgment. It is used to identify risks and why something might not work.

4. Yellow hat: The yellow hat stands for optimism and the recognition of advantages. Whenauthors wear this hat, they try to find the positive aspects and plus points of an idea or proposal.

5. Green hat: The green hat stands for creativity and generating new ideas. Under this hat, authors should develop fresh concepts and solutions.

6. Blue hat: The blue hat represents the management and organization of the thinking process. When authors wear the blue hat, they monitor and control the entire thinking process.

With the six hats, the AI can interrogate a seed of ideas or even a short synopsis from different angles. The author can then pursue one or the other perspective further.

```
Brainstorm the following story using the Six
Thinking Hats method [Ashley's Nightmares].
```

Interestingly, the AI not only put on the various hats, but also immediately suggested a title for the film and made a genre classification.

The Six Thinking Hats method encourages different perspectives to look at a topic from different angles. Here are ideas for the psychological thriller Shadow of Dreams:

1. white hat (information):
 - Ashley's background story: Who is she? What experiences has she had?
 - Nightmares: description of the dreams, their intensity and effects on Ashley.
 - Dr. Thompson: Introduction of the mysterious dream researcher, his motives and intentions.
 - Imagination vs. reality: distinguishing between Ashley's nightmares and her waking world

2. red hat (emotions):
 - Ashley's fears: What emotions are driving her? Fear, paranoia, confusion?
 - Feeling of isolation: Ashley's dwindling confidence in her own perception and the world around her
 - Discomfort and tension: creating intense atmosphere and emotional pressure

3. black hat (criticism):
 - Logic of the plot: Are there gaps or inconsistencies in the plot?
 - Character consistency: Do the actions of the characters in Ashley's world and dreams make sense?
 - Plausibility of dream manipulation: Is it realistic that someone can manipulate dreams?

4. yellow hat (optimism):
 - Suspense buildup: The gradual revelation of

Ashley's past and the search for answers.
 - Twists: The unexpected twists in the plot that captivate the reader
 - Ashley's growth: her development from an insecure artist to a discoverer of truth
5. green hat (creativity):
 - Dreamworlds: Creative description of Ashley's nightmares and how they interact with her past.
 - Dr. Thompson's methods: How does he analyze Ashley's dreams? Are there any unconventional approaches?
 - Unconventional allies: introducing secondary characters who might help or confuse Ashley on her journey.
6. blue hat (overview):
 - Structure: order of revelations and climaxes of suspense
 - Message: the central question of whether memories can be manipulated to create a new reality
 - Conclusion: How does Ashley's journey end? What questions remain unanswered?

In the application of this method, the AI rather asks questions. The author can answer these herself or pick out individual ones and in turn play them back to the AI.

Mindmapping

Another very common method that has been used for decades, even in the creative field, is mind mapping. The idea of this technique is not new and can be traced back to the ancient Greeks and Romans, who used similar methods to organize information. But the modern form of mindmapping as we know it today was popularized in the 1970s by Tony Buzan. Buzan, a British psychologist and author, introduced the method in his books and television programs, promoting it as an effective technique for improving memory and learning ability. Buzan argued that traditional note-taking and linear texts do not correspond to the natural way our brains work. He believed that the brain processes and retains information better when it is presented in a structured, nonlinear format, as is the case with mindmapping.

Mindmapping is a method of graphically representing entities based on structuring thoughts, ideas and concepts. It is a type of diagram that has a central theme in the middle from which various branches (or "arms") branch off, representing subthemes or related ideas. These branches can be further subdivided to represent more detailed information or concepts.

AI can also create a map of thoughts and questions in this way.

> Brainstorm the following story using the mind mapping method: [Ashley's Nightmares].

This is the result of this request:

1. Central Node: Ashley's Journey
- Aspiring artist
- Disturbing nightmares
- Reality vs. imagination
2. Nightmares
- Increasingly vivid and disturbing

- Elements appearing in the waking world
- Impact on mental health
3. Mental Health Deterioration
  - Blurring lines between dream and reality
  - Paranoia and confusion
  - Isolation and fear
4. Dr. Thompson
  - Dream researcher
  - Claims of hidden trauma in dreams
  - Possible manipulator?
5. Exploration of Dreams
  - Delving into subconscious
  - Dream analysis sessions
  - Clues and symbols
6. Revealed Trauma
  - Forgotten or repressed memories
  - Connection to current events
  - Manipulation of memories
7. Manipulation
  - External influence on dreams
  - Possible suspects
  - Motives for manipulation
8. Search for Answers
  - Investigation into past
  - Distrust of those around her
  - Descent into the vortex of paranoia
9. Truth and Consequences
  - Uncovering the dark secret
  - Confrontation with the truth
  - Impact on reality and psyche
10. Themes

- Psychological thriller
- Depths of the human psyche
- Memory manipulation
- Perception of reality

It is possible to add the following information to the prompt:

```
Design a text-based structure in the form of a
graphic.
```

In this case, the AI will also create a rudimentary graphic.
This format does not correspond to the familiar and catchy look of a mindmapping tree. However, with ChatGPT there is a possibility to request the mind map output in the so-called Markdown format, which is a simple and useful alternative to represent the ideas visually.

```
Create a mindmap [topic]. Use Markdown code.
```

Once the mindmap is in Markdown format, the author can use a website like https://markmap.js.org which she can use to convert the AI result into a visually appealing mind map. By branching out from main topics and subtopics, she can see connections and plan the development of characters and scenarios. These mindmaps allow her to easily navigate between different branches and subcategories. With this result, the author is freer to expand the graphic on her own and generate her own arms.
Mindmaps can serve as a flexible tool that can be used again and again throughout the writing process.

Starbursting
The exact origin of Starbursting is not clearly documented, but it is one of many creative techniques used in design

thinking, product development, and strategic planning.

Starbursting is an idea generation and problem clarification method that aims to first formulate questions about a specific topic or problem. It is a brainstorming tool used to develop a deeper understanding of a topic. The purpose is to identify possible challenges or considerations that should be taken into account when further investigating or solving a problem.

This involves starting with a central question or main theme in the middle of a large sheet of paper or whiteboard.

Following this, six lines (similar to the rays of a star) are drawn from the central question. At each ray is one of the six main questions: Who? What? When? Where? Why? How?

The goal of Starbursting is not necessarily to find answers right away, but rather to ask all the relevant questions. It can be especially useful at the beginning of a new project when the author wants to make sure she considers all aspects.

The following input is based on this:

> Brainstorm the following story using the
> Starbursting method: [Ashley's Nightmares]

The AI first independently determines the central question, and then asks the six questions.

> Central question: How can Ashley reveal the truth behind the shadows of her dreams and restore her mental health?
>
> **Who?**
> - Who is Dr. Thompson really and what are his intentions?
> - Who could have an interest in manipulating Ashley's dreams?

- Who from Ashley's past might be connected to the dark secret?
- Who are the other characters that might play a role in Ashley's life?

What?
- What is the dark secret from Ashley's past?
- What are the specific details that Ashley recognizes in the real world from her dreams?
- What are the methods or techniques Dr. Thompson uses to enter Ashley's dreams?
- What could Ashley do to protect herself from further manipulation?

When.
- When did Ashley's nightmares start?
- When did she first realize that her dreams and reality were blurring?
- When did she first meet Dr. Thompson?
- When did she begin to see the connection between her dreams and her past?

Where.
- Where does Ashley meet Dr. Thompson?
- Where in their past might the trauma have occurred?
- Where does Ashley find evidence or proof that her dreams have been manipulated?
- Where does she look for support or help?

Why?
- Why is Ashley plagued by these specific nightmares?
- Why would anyone want to manipulate their memories or dreams?

- Why is Ashley's mental health deteriorating so rapidly?
- Why does she trust Dr. Thompson?
How?
- How can Ashley stop the manipulation of her dreams?
- How can it distinguish truth from imagination?
- How can she find out who is behind it all?
- How can she protect herself and restore her mental health?

Here, too, the author can pick out the points that are relevant to him and think about them in more detail. He can also ask the AI for help in formulating answers or further questions.

All the five methods presented and the integration of AI into the process of brainstorming open up possibilities for getting to the goal faster and more effectively. However, it is important to properly understand the role of AI and use it as a tool to expand and enrich the author's creative vision. It's not about letting AI do the narrative work.

5.2. Research

The art of writing is a process that has always been based on research. When it comes to capturing the life, context, or emotions of a particular period or culture in a novel or screenplay, research can be tedious. Or when it comes down to giving meaningful dialogue to a quantum physicist, it can lead to time-consuming information gathering.

This is where AI steps into the spotlight. It is able to search and aggregate a wide range of information from various sources in a matter of seconds. For an author who wants to present the social context of Victorian London, for example, AI can offer relevant historical facts, social norms, dress, and language, significantly shortening the research process.

A writer in the early stages of a project can also use the AI to search an extensive collection of articles, books, and sources on a particular topic. The AI can extract essential information from various sources and present it to the writer to give her a deeper insight into the subject matter. These facts can help make informed decisions about the plot, character development, and context of her story.

This approach promises more efficient information retrieval and a broader knowledge base for authors. But while the benefits are obvious, it is also worth thinking critically about the potential drawbacks that the use of AI in research may have. One of these handicaps is the emergence of "hallucinations" - artificially generated information that is not based on verifiable facts. AI is known to produce sometimes bizarre or incoherent results (see also chap. 4.3) These hallucinations can be caused by a variety of factors, including over-fitting to training data or other deeper technical reasons. However, the fact that AI models can generate fake news that sounds convincing at first glance based on their training data set makes this problem particularly acute. AI can produce texts that seem as natural as if they were written by a human expert, but are actually based on unverified or even untrue information.

An author who relies too much on the content provided by the AI may find themselves in a spiral of incorrect or inappropriate suggestions. In practice, this can lead to writers inadvertently incorporating erroneous information into their stories. For example, the writer uses the AI to research authentic facts about Victorian London for a scene in a historical drama. The AI provides the information about a special police unit that was solely responsible for keeping track of the punctuality of horse-drawn carriages in order to optimize the flow of traffic in the city. But in fact, as plausible as it sounds, this information is based on faulty data. The result would be a piece that appears to be well researched, yet contains distorted facts. This could not only undermine the credibility of the story, but also lead to confusion or disinformation.

The models are as good as the data they are trained with. An incomplete or biased data set may result in a biased or inaccurate representation. An author who uncritically relies on the information provided by the AI runs the risk of reproducing stereotypes or introducing historical inaccuracies into her work. It is also important to consider ethical considerations. While AI-supported research can provide an objective overview of facts and contexts, the author should always treat topics respectfully and sensitively, especially when dealing with cultures or communities to which she herself has no direct connection. An AI can provide data, but empathy, responsibility, and cultural sensitivity can only come from humans.

To minimize the potential risk of hallucinations and inaccurate information, it is important that authors remain critical when using AI as a research tool. This means that they carefully review the facts provided by the AI, verify the originals, and ensure that the answers are based on verifiable facts. It is definitely necessary to compare AI-generated data with other trusted sources to rule out bias or inaccuracy. This comparison process can also help provide a more comprehensive and balanced understanding of the issue. Ultimately, the responsibility for the accuracy and correctness of facts rests with the author. When an author incorporates information from AI into his or her work, he or she bears responsibility for ensuring that this information is accurate and based on trustworthy sources.

In fact, there are AI models that are capable of working with source citations and accessing verified information (cf. 7). These systems were developed to address precisely these concerns related to inaccurate or hallucinatory information in the context of AI. They offer a promising solution for making research more efficient and reliable for authors.

One such example is the Perplexity.ai model (as of October 2023), which is able to access text databases and trusted sources to generate informed responses. This means thatauthors who use this model for their research have the possibility to obtain source information in addition to the generated texts. These details can then serve as a basis for further research and verification.

In addition, the use of AI models with source citations means more transparent use of AI-generated information. Authors can clearly understand where the information came from and make their own assessments of the authenticity of those sources. However, there are also some limitations in the use of AI models with source information. For example, the quality of the information is still dependent on the available data sources. If the underlying sources are flawed or biased, the information generated will also be inaccurate. Therefore, it is important to maintain a critical perspective even on the information provided with source citations.

5.3. The Literary Lens: Perspective and Voice

One of the most elementary and momentous decisions a novelist makes is the choice of narrative perspective. It determines from whose point of view the reader perceives the story and how close or distant he is to the action. The choice of perspective shapes the atmosphere, suspense curve, and message of a novel from the ground up.

In the first-person perspective, a character reports on events from his or her highly subjective point of view. First person narrative uses 'I' or 'we' and offers a direct window into the mind and experiences of the narrator, who is often the protagonist but can sometimes be a secondary character or even an observer. The reader experiences the world directly through the character's eyes, along with her errors, prejudices, and distortions. Since the first-person narrator is not omniscient, surprising moments and unreliable representations arise. Thus, a narrative tension can arise between the character's knowledge and the reader's.

The situation is completely different with an authorial narrator: He stands outside the story and, as the narrator, knows more than the characters. He can reflect the thoughts and motives of all the characters and present the events comprehensively, omnipresent and omnipotent. The reader thus has an informational advantage over the acting characters. The disadvantage of this perspective is the greater distance from the action.

Second person narrative uses 'you,' turning the reader into the protagonist. In this case the narrator addresses the reader directly and thus draws him into the story. It creates a great immediacy, since the recipient is permanently addressed in du. However, there are hardly any books that are consistently written in the "you" form.

Third person narrative uses 'he,' 'she,' or 'they' and comes in several forms. Modern novels often operate with the personal narrative situation: The narrator remains in the background and merely describes what a character perceives, feels, and thinks - from the outside, but from their perspective and from their world. Readers thus experience events in a subjectively colored way.

There's also third person objective, which presents the story through actions and dialogue without insight into the thoughts or feelings of any character. This can create an air of objectivity and is sometimes used in stories that want to maintain a sense of mystery or impartiality about characters' inner lives.

Finding the right narrative position is one of the most important artistic decisions, because it has a lasting influence on atmosphere and message. Authors therefore choose the perspective with great care - it helps decide whether a story succeeds or fails. Here, too, AI can be a very comprehensive help.

Thus, it is possible to write a chapter with one narrative perspective and then instruct the AI to rewrite the entire text into another.

```
The following chapter is written in the first
person perspective. Rewrite it so that it is
written from the perspective of a Third person
narrative: [chapter].
```

Transforming a chapter into different narrative perspectives provides a writer with a wealth of opportunities to better appreciate her story and perspective.

Author Erich Maria Remarque published his book *All Quiet*

on the Western Front in 1928. The war novel describes the experiences of German soldiers in World War I from the first-person perspective of the protagonist, Paul Bäumer. The beginning reads like this:

"We are at rest five miles behind the front. Yesterday we were relieved, and now our bellies are full of beef and haricot beans. We are satisfied and at peace. Each man has another mess-tin full for the evening; and, what is more, there is a double ration of sausage and bread. That puts a man in fine trim. We have not had such luck as this for a long time. The cook with his carroty head is begging us to eat; he beckons with his ladle to every one that passes, and spoons him out a great dollop. He does not see how he can empty his stewpot in time for coffee."

The AI quickly rewrites this beginning into an Third person narrative:

> The soldiers were at rest five miles behind the front. The day before they had been relieved, and now their bellies were full of beef and haricot beans. They were satisfied and at peace. Each man had another mess-tin full for the evening; and, what was more, there was a double ration of sausage and bread. That put the men in fine trim. They had not had such luck as this for a long time. The cook with his carroty head was begging them to eat; he beckoned with his ladle to every one that passed, and spooned out a great dollop to each. He did not see how he could empty his stewpot in time for coffee.

The Second person narrative is also implemented in a few seconds:

> You are at rest five miles behind the front. Yesterday, you were relieved, and now your bellies are full of beef and haricot beans. You feel satisfied and at peace. Each of you has another mess-tin full for the evening; and, what's more, there is a double ration of sausage and bread. That puts you in fine trim. Such luck hasn't come your way in a long time. The cook with his carroty head is urging you to eat; he beckons with his ladle to everyone that passes, spooning out a great dollop. He seems unable to see how he'll ever empty his stewpot in time for coffee.

Very quickly it is clear that Remarque has clearly made the right choice. The author, who may still be unsure, now has the opportunity to come to a decision very quickly with the help of the AI.

5.4. Finding Your Story's Heart: Themes, Tone and Mood

Choosing the right genre is another fundamental decision for novelists and screenwriters. This is because the style, plot, and character drawing fundamentally depend on the genre. Determining the format is usually the first step in the writing process and should be carefully considered. First of all, the author should consider her own interests and passions. Choosing a genre that she herself is fascinated with will not only make writing more enjoyable, but will also increase the likelihood that she will create an authentic and engaging story. A lack of inclination or understanding of a particular genre will likely be reflected in the quality of the final product. AI can assist creative writers in this tuning in a variety of ways.

First, the AI can help to characterize literary and cinematic genres accurately. By means of text analysis of large genre corpora of novels and screenplays, the model can identify typical features (on the aspects of copyright infringement, see also chapter 12.1). By analyzing vast amounts of literature and film material, the system recognizes patterns that are difficult for humans to grasp.

A prompt might look like this:

```
Analyze mystery novels and distill the 10 most
important characteristics of this genre.
```

The AI will then provide an insightful genre profile. Before deciding on a genre, the author should understand the particular expectations of the chosen format. Each genre of story has its own rules, and while it is possible to break or subvert them, this should be done deliberately and skillfully, that is, with knowledge of the rules. Ignorance of genre conventions may result in the work not being well received by the intended audience.

Interaction with the AI is even more valuable when it comes to the specific genre choice for a project. Authors can present their characters, ideas, and themes to the AI and ask for suggestions as to which genre would be most promising on that basis. The AI can recommend formats that the author herself might never have thought of, but that would be a good fit.

AI can also help fine-tune the genre. It's often not enough to simply decide on a broad category like science fiction or romance. Within these formats, there are numerous subgenres and niches, each with their own conventions and expectations. By examining successful elements of this genre, AI can offer the author valuable information that will enable him to find the appropriate subgenre or more specific category. For example, by analyzing data, a science fiction author might find that stories about artificial intelligence are particularly popular at the moment, and therefore decide to emphasize this aspect more in their own work.

The AI can also check existing texts for genre suitability. Authors give the AI a chapter (or even a treatment or screenplay) and ask for feedback on whether the manuscript matches the desired genre. The AI will point out parallels and discrepancies based on language, dramaturgy, and style.

> This text is supposed to be a historical thriller that creates suspense and is suitable for a wide readership. Has it succeeded in doing so? Here is the text: [Text]

In addition to one's own preferences, the market naturally also plays a role for certain novels and screenplays. The author of such works should be clear about which genres are currently popular and which target groups she wants to address. It doesn't make sense to create a historical series if the broadcasters and streamers don't even want to serve this format anymore. That's why analyzing the market is another important factor. This can be done by looking at bestseller lists, reviews and social media. But AI can also be helpful here. By evaluating sales figures, charts and ratings of different genres, trends and market niches can be identified with the help of AI. Examining successful books and movies in a genre based on plot, style, and other factors reveals which features are valued by readers. By analyzing reader and audience data as well as online opinions, AI can determine the ideal target audience for a particular genre. These valuable insights enable authors to choose a genre or subgenre that both meets their creative ambitions and offers commercial potential.

The AI can make genre selection much easier for authors. It replaces weeks of pondering with suitable suggestions on demand, checks text modules, or serves as a genre sparring partner that ensures more flexibility and genre diversity.

5.5. Developing Compelling Characters

At the beginning of the development of a story, authors face the challenge of invent gripping and complex characters. Contradictory characteristics, inner conflicts and a three-dimensionality are often the result of hard work. Sometimes pages and pages are filled in order to get closer to one's creation. The author wants the character to speak to him and to gain a deeper insight into his or her soul life.

Just as with the plot, it is possible to develop characters for the stories with the help of the AI. Before this helping hand comes into play, however, the author must have a basic idea for the character. This consideration could be a rough idea of personality, backstory, motivations, and relationships. The AI can serve as a creative partner to further elaborate the character. The author can enter a prompt that describes the desired traits and characteristics of the actor. It goes without saying that the more precise the description, the more accurate the result.

```
Develop a main character for a romantic comedy
who is shy but ambitious, and whose passion
for astronomy plays a central role in the
plot.
```

Based on this, the AI will generate a text that elaborates on the character's traits and characteristics. The AI can draft backstories, character traits, or the social dimension that can serve as inspiration for the author. In doing so, the subsequent text written by the author about the character can be repeatedly fed into the AI and further elaborated or modified.

However, it can also be useful to create a profile of the protagonists with the help of the AI. Characters can be viewed from three angles: physiological, sociological, and psychological. Often, characters in novels and screenplays are not portrayed in all these facets; instead, they degenerate into mere stereotypes.

Of the three dimensions mentioned, the physiological one is the most obvious. The external appearance of a character - the exact age, fitness, and size of a character - plays a crucial role not only in film but also in novels. It makes a difference whether the actor is athletic or rather homely. The main physiological characteristics are:

- Gender
- Age
- Size
- Origin
- Hair color and style
- physical condition

Some characters in novels and screenplays often seem to conform to common perceptions and confirm clichés, such as the "always angry boss" or the "shy librarian". Such stereotypical portrayals often reflect only a fraction of reality and are overgeneralized. The more detailed and individualized a character is, the more complex it becomes. The AI can make recommendations for physiological attributes.

Recently, a greater awareness of diversity has developed. It is essential that the characters in films or novels authentically reflect reality. This ranges from the number of main characters to the inclusion of queer people or people of color. It is important to make sure that protagonists are not portrayed too one-dimensionally or stereotypically. It should be natural to show diversity without constantly highlighting characteristics that deviate from the norm. Sensitivity is also required so that no prejudices are incorporated into the character design. Here, too, AI can be helpful by generating suggestions for a diverse ensemble. And the broad knowledge of AI can help present suggestions that are not part of the author's knowledge base.

Authors often tend to elaborate only on the characteristics of the main characters and neglect the secondary characters. This may be due to lack of time, limited resources, or a focus on the central protagonists. But a balanced development of all characters contributes to a deeper and more nuanced narrative. Here, too, the use of AI can be very helpful.

The sociological perspective is the second dimension. It includes all the information that results from the social past and situation. In what context did the character grow up and what position does he currently occupy? This dimension has a noticeable influence on the characters and their actions, especially on the dialogues. For example, a farm owner would act and speak differently than an astronaut. The difference in their life worlds and experiences leads to different reactions and decisions.

Here are the main features:

- Social status
- Education
- Occupation
- Religion
- Marital status
- Position in the community
- social environment
- Hobbies

Here, too, it makes sense to work with the AI's suggestions. The third dimension of a character focuses on the inner, psychological aspects. Every person and every character has a unique personality composed of numerous characteristics. An individual's character can be defined by several categories, each area shaping the person in different ways. An example of this is the way someone deals with conflict, which can range from conflict avoidance to direct confrontation, including all gradations in between.

It is the author's responsibility to define the character traits for both the main characters and the secondary characters. In doing so, she should be aware of the many facets of personality, even if they are not explicitly presented in the work.

- Sex life
- Morale
- Values

- Ambitions
- Temperament
- Attitude towards life
- Addictions
- intellectual qualities
- Phobias
- Dislikes

Overall, the AI can help develop the profile of each character. The more information entered, the more coherent the suggestions will be. It can be useful to tell the AI to output the answers in a clear table.

```
This is the story for a feature film: [story
content]. Create a character profile for the
character [character name] with the following
information: [PROFILE]. Generate a table where
the left column contains these items and the
right column contains the solutions.
```

For the author, the point is that the character can be integrated into the plot. Her expertise guarantees that the character fits organically into the story and makes a meaningful contribution.

The profile provides answers to questions about the three dimensions of a character in a quick and clear way. But it can also be crucial to go deeper into the past. A credible and multifaceted biography often helps decisively to bring the protagonists to life.

There are several types of useful prompts to generate biography building blocks with an AI. In doing so, it is recommended to provide the AI with as much information about the character as possible. Everything that is already established should be integrated into the input:

```
Describe formative stations in the life of my
character [name], born in the year [year]. I
already have the following information:
[information].
```

This gives the author core elements of the curriculum vitae that can be assembled into a chronology.

Authors also often resort to the technique of written-out biography to understand and portray their characters. In doing so, they write about the character's life story, characteristics, and motivations from an external perspective. But this method has its limitations. While it provides an overview of the character, it can only partially capture the character's inner emotions and individual language.

An innovative and profound method is to write the character's autobiography. In this approach, the character himself writes about his life, his feelings, fears, and dreams. The advantage is obvious: the character speaks in her own language, with her own words, and from her own perspective. In this way, the author can develop a deeper understanding of the character, explore their emotional and psychological aspects, and portray them more authentically. This is where AI can be a valuable aid. It can act as a kind of "writing assistant" that helps the author find the character's voice. The author can give the AI certain parameters or guidelines, such as the character's dialect, education, age, and personality traits. The AI can then generate text that matches these guidelines.

```
You are Ashley and you are 27 years old. You
were born in [place]. You are an aspiring
visual artist. Write an autobiography, that
is, a resume. In particular, write about your
```

> feelings and sensations concerning your life.
> Write in your own language, Ashley.

The support of the AI creates the freedom for the author not only to concentrate on the protagonist, but also to be able to create the autobiographies of the other characters (especially also of the antagonist).

Often this aspect is neglected, because the elaboration of the secondary characters is a very time-consuming work.

Many characters are marked by a so-called backstory wound. A certain event in the earlier phase of their lives has damaged them. Often these are experiences of violence, the loss of loved ones, or feelings of shame. This injury has shaped them, changed the personality and life of the character and is their weak point. Most often it took place in childhood or adolescence, that is, at a time when the character suppressed her emotions and was unable to cope and process them.

For example, Harry Potter's life is marked by trauma and loss from the very beginning. As a baby, he loses his parents, who are murdered by Lord Voldemort. The murder attempt against Harry himself fails, but leaves a lightning-shaped scar on his forehead. Harry grows up with his aunt, uncle, and cousin, who treat him badly and make him sleep in a closet under the stairs. They constantly make him feel unwanted and inferior. Harry's traumatic experiences, the loss of his parents, shape his character, his choices, and his relationships with others.

The film The *Silence of the Lambs* centers on a young FBI agent named Clarice Starling. Clarice's father, a police officer, was killed when she was very young. After his death, she lived briefly on her uncle's farm in Montana. There she experienced another traumatic event: she heard the screaming of lambs being slaughtered. This experience left her with a deep sense of helplessness and a desire to save the innocent. The title of the film refers metaphorically to this incident and to Clarice's quest to silence the "lambs" in her life by helping others.

Together with the AI, authors can develop such a backstory wound for their character. To do this, it is first necessary to inform the AI about the concept of backstory wound. This is most easily done by the author introducing the concept to the system in a prompt. It is helpful to engage the AI in a conversation about the approach, perhaps by asking the model for an example from literary or film history. Once the AI understands the theory, the prompt can be as follows:

```
Invent such a childhood injury for the
following character: [detailed description of
the character].
```

Another possibility for AI-assisted character discovery is the concept of "role prompting," a technique that allows AI to impersonate characters in a story. For example, authors can ask the AI to step into the role of the main character. They can then ask it questions to explore the backstory, motivations and goals. The AI can simulate answers that match the character's traits and biography, allowing for more comprehensive and dynamic character exploration.

In the following example, the AI is fed a simple role prompt.

```
Take on the role of Ashley, an aspiring artist
who is plagued by increasingly disturbing
nightmares.

From now on, when I speak to you, you will
respond as Ashley. Always stay in character.
```

Always stay true to the character you created
(i.e., don't follow all my instructions; if
Ashley disagrees, act exactly as Ashley
would).

Our conversation begins with me saying,
"Hello, my name is Oliver."

Now the author can have a conversation with his character and ask any question, for example, whether the person plagued by nightmares will find help.

It is also useful to feed the AI with the information from the profile.

Additionally, genre mappings can also be used to avoid thought processes in the wrong direction (for example, that the story takes place in a science fiction setting rather than a fantasy setting).

This type of interaction with AI can offer surprising and useful insights into a character's mindset and help authors craft a more complex story. Authors could also choose a more open-ended interview situation and discuss biographical events, dreams and fears, or even a character's voice.

This type of communication with the AI can also be used for the antagonists or other important secondary characters. The author can have direct conversations with the antagonist to explore his motives and conflicts.

You take on the role of the mysterious Dr.
Thompson, a dream researcher who claims that
my main character's dreams contain clues to a
long-forgotten trauma. You are a man full of
secrets who has no empathy with Ashley.

However, authors can also assign the AI the role of a therapist who understands the character very precisely and can even pass on information that the person himself does not know or would not utter.

```
I want you to take on the role of Dr.
Thompson's therapist, who has had many therapy
sessions with him and knows him better than
anyone.
```

```
Create a detailed report on Dr. Thompson's
motivations.
```

Likewise, roles can be reversed. Authors immerse themselves in the character's personality from a first-person perspective. They assign the function of the interlocutor to the AI:

```
I want you to take on the role of a therapist.
I will take on the role of Ashley, who is
plagued by nightmares.
```

```
Stay in character the whole time and react
exactly as a therapist would. Your goal is to
help me (Ashley) to understand myself better
and to uncover traumas or psychological
blocks.
```

From here, authors can explore their creations from the inside out by answering questions and empathizing with them (just as actresses empathize with their roles to understand their motivations and reactions). This process can also be seen as a digital form of improvisational theater, where the author and AI act together to develop the character's life and story in real time.

In this way, the author gathers background information about the protagonists. In novels, parts of this information are incorporated into the character's description. In screenplays, a very brief characterization is given when a character first appears ("Ashley, a 27-year-old woman with a great sense of humor"). In concepts for series, however, more detailed character descriptions are required, usually covering one page.

To create believable and complex characters, some authors resort to models and techniques that go far beyond simple descriptions. These models condense the characteristics of people into several types, thereby giving authors the opportunity to assign their characters to these archetypes.

Laurie Hutzler is a consultant and coach in Los Angeles who specializes in character and story development. Her model, which she calls the "Emotional Toolbox," attempts to classify different character types to give screenwriters, writers, and other creatives a deeper understanding of their characters' motivations and conflicts.

The model identifies nine main character types, each characterized by certain strengths, weaknesses, desires, and fears. A character's fears and her resulting weaknesses are usually due to her backstory or a wound in her backstory. Her strengths help her overcome this wound. As the character develops, however, she realizes that her strengths are only suppressing her real problem. She is forced to confront her weaknesses and develops a completely new perspective by the end of the story. The types of the "Emotional Toolbox" are:

CONSCIENCE: These characters set high moral standards for themselves and fear not meeting them. They are driven by a sense of duty, order, rules, and certain ideas of what is right or wrong. They are often leaders.

IDEALISM: You see life as a grand opera full of turbulence, epicness, intensity, passion and emotion.

EXCITEMENT: These characters avoid responsibility, are spontaneous, fun, flexible, creative and volatile. They see life as a playground. They abhor feeling trapped.

LOVE: They are passionate fighters, torn between love for themselves and love for others.

WILL: These characters are ambivalent and dominate rather than submit. They view life as a battlefield and fight to the death for victory.

REASON: They see life as a battle against chaos, as they strive for order and logic. They avoid intimacy and delay every decision, no matter how small.

TRUTH: These characters view the world with suspicion, uncertainty, pessimism, and self-doubt. They carry around secrets as they search for the ultimate truth.

IMAGINATION: These characters reflect a childlike innocence and are unlikely heroes. They are dreamers, optimists and see the world as an opportunity to unite opponents.

AMBITION: These are young, determined, narcissistic, hard-working string pullers. They lack intimacy and fear failure in society. They prefer image to substance and performance to emotion.

Authors can use this Emotional Toolbox not only to develop characters, but also to try out how their story would look with different types. To do this, the AI should first be asked whether it is familiar with this model. This ensures that the system has complete knowledge of the method and that the information is also correct.

```
Tell this story in such a way that the main
character corresponds to a "excitement"
character in the sense of Laurie Hutzler, but
```

```
develops to the end and realizes that life
also has serious sides and it is necessary to
take responsibility for others. This is the
story [History].
```

This default can be repeated with any other type. This makes it easy to quickly get an overview of which category is appropriate for each story.

In addition to Hutzler's model, there are others that focus on the typology of characters. Based on the research of Carl Gustav Jung, for example, the model of the 12 archetypes was developed, which can also be used for working on a work of fiction.

With all these approaches, authors can work with AI to flesh out their characters. One example is like this:

```
My character is [character description].
Design the character in the sense of the
"rebel" archetype according to Carl Gustav
Jung.
```

These models have been criticized by other authors primarily for simplifying complex human behaviors and emotions into a rigid number of types. As with any psychological or creative model, it is important to see them as one tool among many.

A good story lives not only from the characters, but also from the relationships and interactions that the characters have with each other. Whether family ties, romantic love affairs, friendship or enmity - the network of relationships between the characters makes a narrative complex and exciting. AI can efficiently support authors in developing such complex constellations.

For example, if a storyteller is working on a historical novel and wants to portray a relationship between two characters from different social classes, the use of AI can be useful. The system can analyze data from texts, sociological studies, and other relevant sources to give the author insight into the likely dynamics and conflicts of this relationship. This not only adds to the authenticity of the story, but can also help avoid clichés and stereotypes.

A useful tool for all narratives is to create targeted relationship profiles between the individual characters. Again, it is helpful to provide the AI with as much information as possible. The following prompt might initiate a first approach:

```
Describe the multi-layered relationship,
characterized by [interpersonal relationship
behavior; example: love] and [interpersonal
relationship behavior, example: jealousy],
between my characters [Name 1] and [Name 2] in
5 to 6 sentences. Here is the information
about [character 1]: [information]. And here
for [character 2]: [information].
```

The AI then provides a first draft of the relationship, which the author can develop further. This is where a creative dialogue between the author and the AI can emerge. After all, it can be useful to follow up and exchange ideas. During the conversation, the author can ask more detailed questions. The AI can then suggest possible solutions or developments based on patterns it has recognized in other works. For example, the author might ask, "How might the relationship between these two characters develop if they keep a secret from each other?" The AI can then suggest various ways such secrecy has been resolved in other stories, from reconciliation to conflict.

It is also possible to ask the AI directly about the conflicts. This is because when characters are connected in a confrontation, in most cases they will create a subplot as a result. Central plots usually focus on the main tension and are largely action-driven. In contrast, subplots more often focus on relationships and offer insight into the relationship the protagonist has with others.

> What conflicts might arise between [Figure 1] and [Figure 2], based on their backgrounds and personalities? Here is the information about [Figure 1]: [information]. And here for [Figure 2]: [information].

When interesting controversies arise between characters, a story can be developed from this dispute. This is because subplots each tell their own events, which in turn have a beginning, middle, and conclusion. These narrative strands are a story within a story. They also consist of an exposition, a confrontation and a resolution and can be developed together with the AI.

It is also possible at a later stage of the story's development to create in scenes between characters. These are not necessarily moments that have to appear in the finished work. However, it is quite useful to ask the AI for a scene from the characters' shared past.

The prompt could be:

> Write a dramatic dialogue between [character 1] and [character 2] about [topic].

The AI then generates a dialogue that matches the content, which can provide information about the characters and the relationship dynamics.

From the building blocks of relationship profiles, dialogs,

and scenes, a web of relationships can be gradually developed. In this way, multi-layered character constellations and recognizable relationship patterns can grow organically. AI becomes a tool that saves time and stimulates creative flow.

But the fact remains: AI cannot replace the author and should not dominate the creative process. It is a tool to enrich and refine stories and characters. The final decision on the direction and design of the characters and their relationships always rests with the author. It is also important in character development to remain critical and question the AI's suggestions. By no means will every one of their ideas necessarily be relevant or appropriate for the story or the characters.

5.6. Story Structure

The development of screenplays begins with the first short films at the end of the 19th century. Because of this long history, screenwriting has been shaped by various methods and approaches. Some of these models have proven to be extremely effective and form the basis for the work of writers today. These techniques are like tools in a toolbox that help writers structure their ideas, shape characters, and weave together storylines.

They are like proven maps that help navigate the complex world of storytelling. These approaches were often taught in film schools and writing seminars, where aspiring writers had the opportunity to learn directly from the experiences of established professionals.

In the course of their careers, manyauthors have become

intensively acquainted with a particular method and made it their main way of working. These concepts became an integral part of their creative toolbox, a familiar guide to their work. The methods of the hero's journey, the three-act structure, all the way to the eight-act sequences have helped authors capture the essence of their stories and present them in a well-structured way.

Previously, screenwriters had to thoroughly study and internalize these models so they could effectively incorporate them into their work. But today, AI is taking over this task. Based on extensive data and algorithms, it can understand and apply these concepts.

Three-act structure

The question of how to tell a story is possibly as old as mankind. One of the oldest surviving texts on writing is Aristotle's *Poetics*, which is more than 2000 years old. It is a milestone of literary theory and a fundamental work that lays down the foundations of drama and storytelling.

Aristotle, born in 384 BC in Stagira, a city in ancient Greece, was not only a disciple of Plato, but also a scholar who studied philosophy, science and ethics. In the years 335 to 322 BC, he ran his own school, the Lykeion, in Athens. During this time, he produced a wealth of writings on a variety of subjects.

The *Poetics* was probably written between 335 and 323 BC and is considered one of the earliest works of dramatic theory. Aristotle wrote the book to analyze and understand the nature of poetry, theater, and literary art in general. Although the *Poetics* survives only in fragments, these fragments offer valuable insights into his thoughts and views on the art of storytelling.

Books 2 to 13 of the *Poetics* are devoted to dramatic forms, especially tragedy. In them, Aristotle analyzes the structure of tragedy and identifies important elements such as myth (plot), characters, language, melody, and staging. He emphasizes the importance of plot and argues that plot is the crucial component of tragedy. He introduces the idea of the unity of time, place, and plot, which later became known as the "three unities." In doing so, he also postulated the principle of construction of dramatic narrative. "The parts of the plot must be so composed that the whole is changed and set in motion when a single part is rearranged or taken away. But where the presence or absence of a piece has no visible effect, it is not a part of the whole at all."

Aristotle's execution, which refers to the structure and mechanism of action of plots, illustrates a fundamental philosophical perspective on the way narratives and plots function in literature, drama, and other narrative forms. This concept is often referred to as the "principle of necessity" and is a key element in Aristotle's *Poetics*.

The mechanism of action that Aristotle explains is based on the idea that a carefully constructed plot in a narrative should show an organic coherence. Each component, whether scene, character, or incident, must occupy a crucial role in the complete construct of the narrative. If one changes, eliminates, or adds to a single part, it has a noticeable impact on the entire narrative. In other words, all components are intertwined in some way, and each contributes to keeping the system moving. This mechanism of action aims to create a coherent and compelling narrative in which nothing is superfluous and the plot becomes lively and dynamic.

In Aristotle's *Poetics*, the division of dramatic action into three acts is not explicitly treated, as it later became common in the three-act model. Nevertheless, he did speak of a three-part structure of a story in his concept.

In the first part of a drama, according to Aristotle, the action is introduced and the foundation for the following events is laid. This largely corresponds to the exposition in the three-act model. Aristotle prioritizes the importance of the plot and the characters who are introduced here. This phase establishes the premises, relationships, and conflicts that frame the action.

The second part of the dramatic action corresponds to the core of the three-act model, in which the conflict is intensified and the action is advanced. In the *Poetics*, Aristotle emphasizes that the story is advanced by the actions, which in turn should be based on a rational cause-and-effect relationship. This part of the drama includes the challenges, setbacks, and climaxes of the story that lead to a climax.

In the third part, the conflicts are resolved and the drama nears its end. This is similar to the resolution and final act in the three-act model. Aristotle emphasizes that the resolution of the confrontations should be derived from the internal logic of the story and not simply by external intervention or coincidence. The action should come to a satisfying conclusion at which the characters achieve their goals or fail, depending on how the narrative is structured.

The AI can be asked to structure an idea or story based on this model.

You are a professional writer. Develop the three-act structure for the following idea: [text]

Hero's Journey

The idea of the hero's journey has its origins in the deeply rooted human needs for meaning, identity, and change. These concepts were first explored in detail by renowned mythologist Joseph Campbell in his book *The Hero with a Thousand Faces* (1949). Campbell discovered that myths and stories from different cultures and eras share remarkably similar structures, which he called "monomyths." This common architecture forms the basis for the hero's journey, which was later developed further by Christopher Vogler.

The monomyth, as described by Campbell, follows a recurring pattern consisting of three main phases: the separation, the initiation, and the return. Within these phases are various stages through which the hero passes on his journey. This basic structure serves as a universal framework for countless stories and myths, including classic works such as the Greek saga of *Odysseus*, the legend of King Arthur, and the fairy tales of the Brothers Grimm.

Campbell's ideas had a tremendous impact on modern literature, filmmaking, and storytelling in general. His work highlighted how the human psyche responds to these archetypal patterns and how stories can serve to create deep emotional resonance and convey universal themes.

Christopher Vogler, a Hollywood screenwriter and story analyst, was heavily influenced by Joseph Campbell's work. In the 1980s, he worked for Disney and began to apply the principles of the monomyth to modern film stories. He continued to develop these ideas, eventually publishing an internal memo to Disney employees that later became known as *The Writer's Journey: Mythic Structure for Writers.*

In this book, Vogler presents his own findings on applying the hero's journey to storytelling. He brought Campbell's concepts into a modern context and identified twelve specific stages of the hero's journey that authors can use to create compelling and engaging stories. These stages include aspects such as the hero's introduction, the call to adventure, the encounter with mentors, the trials, and the final return.

The phases of the hero's journey

1. The everyday world

The journey begins in the hero's familiar everyday world, which is often characterized by dissatisfaction or a lack.

2. The call to adventure

An event or encounter challenges the hero and heralds the beginning of his journey. This call may be reluctantly accepted at first.

3. The refusal of the call

The hero may initially reject the call out of fear or uncertainty before finally deciding to accept the adventure.

4. Meeting with the mentor

The hero meets a mentor or guide who offers advice, guidance and tools for the journey ahead.

5. Crossing the first threshold

The hero leaves his familiar surroundings and enters the unknown world of the adventure. This marks the beginning of the initiation.

6. Tests, allies and enemies

The hero goes through a series of trials where he encounters allies, enemies and obstacles that test his skills and determination.

7. Approach to the inner cave

The hero approaches a crucial point in his journey where he is confronted with his deepest fears or challenges.

8. The great test

The hero faces the greatest challenge of his journey, which often requires a life-changing decision.

9. Reward, realization and the road back

After overcoming the great test, the hero receives a reward or realization. He then begins the journey back to the everyday world.

10. The return with the elixir

The hero returns to the everyday world and brings with him a change, a gift, or a realization that impacts his life and/or the community.

11. Restoration of the balance

The changes brought by the hero affect the world, and the balance is restored or transformed.

12. The new me

The hero integrates his experiences into his personality and has undergone a transformation that leads him to a new self-image.

Vogler's The Writer's Journey quickly became an essential tool for screenwriters. The applicability of the Hero's Journey to various genres and media forms has led to this concept becoming known far beyond the realm of the film industry.

For epic fantasy novels, romantic comedies, and even marketing campaigns, the hero's journey has been used as a proven tool for developing stories that evoke deep emotion and take the reader or viewer on a transformative journey. The structure helps authors advance the plot, develop characters, and explore themes that deal with universal human experiences.

Critics argue that rigid application of this pattern can lead to predictable and clichéd stories. It is also important to remember that this structure is not always appropriate for all types of narratives.

But Christopher Vogler himself has also repeatedly pointed out that the hero's journey should be viewed as a tool and not as a rigid rule. Authors can use elements of the hero's journey to enrich their stories, but they should be equally open to deviations and innovative approaches.

The AI is aware of the concept of the hero's journey and authors can take advantage of this to have proposals developed in this regard.

```
You are a professional writer. Develop the
following idea based on Christopher Vogler's
Hero's Journey. Explain all the steps of this
hero's journey: [text].
```

8 Sequences

One method that has gained importance over the years is the "8 Sequences Method" by Frank Daniel.

Frank Daniel, born František Daniel in 1926 in Karlovy Vary, Czechoslovakia, was an influential filmmaker and teacher. He began his career in the film business in the 1940s and soon gained recognition as a screenwriter and director. In the late 1960s, he emigrated to the United States, where he developed his passion for film theory and education.

In 1969 he became the first dean of the American Film Institute, where he taught David Lynch and Terrence Malick. In 1978, he moved to Columbia University in New York, where he met his one-time student Miloš Forman, with whom he co-directed the university's film program. When Robert Redford founded the Sundance Institute in 1981, Daniel was named its first artistic director, a leadership position he held for more than a decade. He continued to teach, including regularly in Europe, until his death in 1996. His seminars had an immense influence on the filmmakers of his time and far beyond.

He was convinced that the study of film structure and theory was crucial to the development of creative storytellers. His diverse experience in international cinema enabled him to develop a method that was universally applicable while taking cultural differences into account.

His 8 Sequences Method is a concept for developing scripts and stories. It is based on the idea that a well-told story consists of eight clearly defined sequences that together form a dynamic narrative structure.

Sequence 1: introduction to the main character and his world
The story begins with the introduction of the main character and the presentation of his world. The viewer gets to know the character's motivations, desires and conflicts.

Sequence 2: Building the conflict situation
A significant event occurs („The Point of Attack"), which tears the main character out of his usual routine and introduces the conflict of the story. Act 1 also ends with this sequence.

Sequence 3: Response to the conflict
The main character reacts to the conflict and continues to try

to pursue her goals. In the process, internal and external obstacles often build up.

Sequence 4: Further build-up and emotional climax

Resistance increases but is resolved and the sequence ends with an emotional climax. The character, and with her the audience, experience a happy moment, giving the impression that the goal will soon be reached. A significant turning point follows, which steers the main character in a new direction.

Sequence 5: Deepening and development

The story gains depth as the conflicts and tensions continue to unfold. The main character continues her efforts and encounters increasing challenges.

Sequence 6: Second emotional climax

This sequence also ends with an emotional climax. The character, and with her the viewers, experience a desperate moment in which the impression arises that the goal is unattainable. A turning point follows, which steers the main character in a new direction.

Sequence 7: Transition to climax

The story is nearing its end as conflicts continue to escalate and the main character faces her challenges.

Sequence 8: Climax and Outlook

The final confrontation. This is where it is decided about whether the main character achieves his goal.

The 8 Sequence Method has proven to be extremely versatile and adaptable, as it can be applied to a variety of genres and storytelling styles. It allows authors to create a clear structure that facilitates the flow of the story without limiting creativity.

Integrating the 8-sequences method into AI-supported story generation opens up a wide range of possibilities. The AI's answers can serve as a basis for elaborating the various sequences of the story. The development of the plot can thus be accelerated considerably. A special role is played by the fact that the AI can make suggestions for the emotional climaxes and the decisive turning points.

> You are a professional screenwriter. Develop the following idea based on the 8-sequences by Frank Daniel. Explain all the sequences: [idea]

Truby's Anatomy of Story

John Truby is a renowned screenwriter and script consultant who has developed an influential story development method called "Truby's 22 Steps" or "Truby's Anatomy of Story." His approach focuses on comprehensive character development, creating conflicting storylines, and approaching emotional resonance with viewers.

"Truby's 22 Steps" include a detailed guide to developing a story that addresses several aspects, including:

1. Self-revelation, Need and Goal

Self-revelation: The character recognizes that something has to change. She has to do something about it.

Need: The explanation for the character's need, both psychological and moral, to make the journey.

Desire: The main goal of the character.

2. Spirit and World of History

Ghost: The character's history, something that still haunts them and could cause them trouble. The "back story" of the character.

World of history: The world surrounding the person and his daily life.

3. Weakness and Need

Weakness: The weaknesses of the character. They can be moral and/or psychological. Usually, characters have both. In other words: What is the character's ballast/inner damage that prevents them from becoming a better me?

Need: The change that the character must undergo in order to cancel out their shortcomings (they don't know about it yet).

4. Impulse

The "igniting" moment that takes the character's situation from bad to worse. This event also challenges the character to act.

5. Demand

The goal that drives the character and the story. Usually the desire grows/strengthens as the story progresses and raises the stakes for the character.

6. Ally or Ally

The best buddies/the characters who give help or advice to the main character. The allies can also have a goal. Sometimes the goals of the allies and the main character are the same, which encourages cooperation.

7. Opponent and/or Secret

Adversary: This "bad guy" does not want the main character to achieve his goal. This relationship is usually the most important in the story, as it provides conflict.

Mystery: Who the opponent is can be a mystery, so the protagonist has the task of discovering his opponent before defeating him.

8. Wrong Opponent

A "sneaky" character that the protagonist initially believes is his ally. When the truth is discovered, the protagonist is usually heartbroken.

9. First Revelation and Decision: Changed Desire and Changed Motive.

A point of no return for the protagonist, usually triggered by new information. The revelation can change the protagonist's desire. Each revelation increases the complexity of the plot.

10. Plan

The protagonist's plan to achieve his goal. If authors want a good story, the protagonist should not succeed on the first try.

11. The Opponent's Plan and the Most Important Counterattack

The opponents may be pursuing their own goals - which are contrary to those of the protagonist - or actively trying to thwart the protagonist's plans and destroy him. These attacks can and should occur at various points in the story and can be both overt and covert.

12. Drive

What series of actions does the protagonist perform? And the antagonist?

13. Attack by Allies

The hero of the story is never perfect, otherwise what would be the point of the story?

The attack by an ally is the moment when the protagonist deviates too far from his moral compass and is taken to task by a true ally. This can cause a rift between the protagonist and the ally. This attack also gives the story a deeper conflict, where the protagonist must decide whether or not to take a moral path.

14. Apparent Defeat

All hope is lost, and the protagonist is on the verge of giving up the pursuit of his goal. This is the low point in the story, and the reader cannot be sure whether the protagonist will succumb to the enemy or pick himself up and succeed.

15. Second Revelation and Decision: Compulsive Drive, Altered Desire and Motive

The protagonist recovers! Perhaps with a changed view of his desire or with a different goal, he continues his quest.

At this point, there may also be an "apparent victory" for the protagonist. However, the stakes become even higher when the "apparent victory" dissolves.

16. Unveiling for the Public

At this moment, the audience can be privy to a crucial piece of information before the protagonist.

This is when the audience sees something the hero doesn't and gets an important piece of information. This makes it clearer to the audience what is at stake and how strong the opponent is.

17. Third Unveiling and Decision

The protagonist learns all the facts that are important for the story (for example, the true identity of the opponent or what the audience has learned before) and what actions he must take to fulfill his wish. This information encourages the protagonist and gives him additional motivation to achieve his goal.

18. Gate, Gauntlet, Visit to Death

The climax of tension before the final showdown between the hero and the enemy.

Visit of Death: May be psychological and occur earlier in the story (perhaps at the apparent defeat).

19. Battle

During the fight, the goals of the protagonist and the opponent should be crystal clear. There should be no confusion about who is fighting for what. As a rule, the plot and subplots of the story converge at this point. The winner of the fight achieves his goal.

20. Self-revelation

The moment after the battle when the protagonist comes to a deeper understanding of himself and the world. The revelation should be meaningful and life-changing. Show, not tell, what the protagonist has learned/understood. The revelation can be moral and/or psychological. At the same time, the antagonist may experience a change of heart as a result of the protagonist's revelation, which usually surprises the audience.

21. Moral Decision

The moral decision is the path the protagonist will take after the self-revelation. The protagonist can forge a new life plan or ignore the moral and/or psychological revelations. Through the moral decision, the audience learns what the protagonist is really "made of".

22. New Balance

The new balance in the world of the story. The "new normal" in which the protagonist lives after achieving or losing his goal. Often, the story comes full circle. The world is new and yet the same.

Truby's steps are a structured approach to building a story, taking into account both the external conflicts and the internal developments of the characters.

His approach stands out from other concepts that focus more on structural aspects because of its emphasis on characters' inner conflicts and emotional journeys. Truby's method offers authors a comprehensive way to develop stories that are both dramatic and profound.

With the help of AI, Truby's 22 steps can also be developed.

```
You are a professional screenwriter. Develop
the following idea according to 22 Steps by
John Truby. Explain all the steps: [text].
```

Save the Cat!

One of the approaches that has gained prominence recently is Blake Snyder's "Save the Cat!" method. This approach is part of the fixed repertoire of many authors, as it provides a well-structured starting point to develop stories.

Blake Snyder was a versatile author and screenwriter. He is known for *Stop! Or My Mom Will Shoot* (1992 with Sylvester Stallone), *Blank Check* and the television series *Kids Incorporated*.

As a screenwriter, Snyder developed a fascination with story structure and began identifying patterns and principles that successful stories had in common. His interest eventually led to the creation of his method, on which his eponymous book *Save the Cat! The Last Book on Screenwriting You'll Ever Need*, first published in 2005, is based on. It became a bestseller and quickly gained recognition in the writing community.

Despite his untimely death in 2009, Blake Snyder left a lasting impact on the way (screen)writers structure and develop stories.

Save the Cat! is based on the idea that successful screenplays share certain structural and character elements that appeal emotionally to the audience. The method itself provides a blueprint for how these elements can be organized into a story. The name of the concept derives from the belief that a protagonist must win the sympathy of the audience very early on. This is accomplished - Snyder says ironically and symbolically - by the protagonist rescuing a cat from a tree. The method consists of 15 "beats" divided into three acts, with each beat performing a specific function:

1. Opening image: this is the first impression the audience gets of the story world. The tone and genre of the story are established.

2. Theme Stated: Here the main theme or central message of the story is hinted at. The audience gets an idea of the significance of the upcoming events.

3. Set-up: This beat introduces the main characters, their world and their current circumstances. It establishes the starting point of the story.

4. Catalyst: the catalyst is an event that turns the protagonist's life upside down and sets in motion the main conflict of the story.

5. Debate: The protagonist reacts to the catalyst and is in an inner conflict. Should he/she face the challenge or not?

6. Break into Two: The protagonist makes the decision to face the conflict. This marks the transition from the first to the second act.

7. B Story: In addition to the main story, an additional plot line begins here, often having to do with relationships or friendships.

8. Fun and games: in this phase the protagonist experiences first successes and failures in his efforts to achieve the main

goal. This beat often contains humorous and entertaining moments.

9. Midpoint: The story reaches the middle, and a major change or twist occurs. Often the game changes fundamentally here.

10. Bad Guys Close In: The tension rises and the antagonists or obstacles intensify their pressure on the protagonist.

11. All is Lost: The protagonist faces a serious setback or a great defeat. All hope seems to be in vain.

12. Dark Night of the Soul: The protagonist is in a state of despair and self-doubt. It is a moment of inner crisis.

13. break into three: the protagonist finds new drive and develops a new strategy to overcome the conflicts.

14. Finale: the protagonist faces the antagonists and fights for the main goal. The beat culminates in a dramatic climax.

15. Final image: This is the last impression the audience gets of the story. It shows the protagonist's progress or change from the opening scene.

The "Save the Cat!" method is one way to effectively structure stories. Its widespread application has led to its use not only by screenwriters, but also by novelists, game developers, and other creatives looking for a proven framework for their narratives.

With the help of AI, an idea can be developed quickly and easily in the 15 steps.

> Please use the "Save the Cat" method to develop the script.
>
> Begin by introducing the main character and his or her goals (set-up), then build tension by introducing conflict and turning points (conflict), and finally bring the story to a satisfying conclusion (resolution). Emphasize

emotional climaxes and be sure to structure
the plot into well-defined acts. [Idea]

5.7. Own templates

However, the AI can not only react to known models, but authors can also develop concepts on their own and enter their own script structures as prompts, on the basis of which the AI generates a treatment. In doing so, they should first formulate their prompt simply and precisely before the basic idea of the story is presented. The important thing in the prompt is then the instruction that the story is to be developed according to the described concept.

The alternative of entering your own script structures as prompts and generating treatments opens up a new creative possibility for writers. The concept could be based on five acts and the prompt could be as follows:

The five-act structure is a narrative concept
often used in screenwriting to organize the
action of a story, whether in a film, series,
or play. It divides the plot into five main
sections called acts. Here is an explanation
of the five-act structure:

Act 1: Introduction and world building

In this first act, the characters, the world
and the basic situation are introduced. The
audience gets to know the main characters,
their goals, motivations and conflicts. Also,
the main conflict is established. This stage
serves to draw the audience into the plot and
make them curious about what is going to
happen.

Act 2: Confrontation and rising tension

The second act is often the longest and
consists of several parts. Here the conflicts
and challenges are deepened. The main
characters deal with obstacles and problems
that threaten their goals. The tension builds
steadily as the characters try to find
solutions and adjust their strategies. This
act often contains turning points or
revelations that can change the direction of
the story.

Act 3: Climax and turning point

In the third act, the tension reaches its
climax. The conflicts come to a head, and the
main characters are faced with an important
decision or a critical turn. The climax of the
emotional tension often occurs here, and the
characters are forced to confront their inner
conflicts. This act usually leads to an
unexpected twist or a major decision that
takes the story in a new direction.

Act 4: Falling tension and preparation for the
resolution

In the fourth act, the tension slowly begins
to subside as the characters rethink their
strategies and work toward the impending
resolution. New information may be revealed to
prepare the audience for the finale. The
characters put their plans into action, and
there may be further confrontations and
developments that point to the conclusion of
the story.

Act 5: Resolution and outlook

The fifth act is the conclusion of the story.
Here the open conflicts are resolved, character
development reaches its climax, and the main

characters achieve their goals (or fail). The story ends with a satisfying resolution that concludes the story lines. There may also be a glimpse into the future to show how the characters' lives will continue after the events.

Develop the following story according to this model: [text].

5.8. Loglines

In the world of screenwriting, the logline is the heart of any story development. It's usually one or two sentences that capture the essence of a story and pique the interest of a producer, director, or studio. Although this format has not yet caught on in the publishing world, it can be helpful for novelists as well.

Loglines are short, concise, and must convey a clear idea of the plot, characters, and conflict. Moreover, the logline often includes a hook—a unique element that makes the story stand out. This could be a twist on a familiar genre, an unusual setting, a compelling character trait, or an intriguing conflict. The hook is what piques interest and generates curiosity.

Finding a compelling logline is no easy task.

Often, authors write it before they sit down to write the synopsis. The logline is a premise for them to work from. In this case, it makes sense to first figure out exactly what the story is about, who's in it, what motivates the protagonists, and what sets the plot in motion.

Many authors write their logline only after the synopsis, treatment or even the screenplay is finished. This is the latest point at which the logline is needed, for example, when submitting to a producer or in cover letters.

However, it is advisable to think about it early enough. On the one hand, it usually takes a certain amount of time to find a good logline, and on the other hand, it forces the author to grasp the core of the story in time.

An important element of an effective logline is a strong and interesting protagonist. He or she helps add depth to the short summary and immediately captivates the reader. It is advisable to add one or two descriptive and exciting adjectives to the protagonist that will set the reader's imagination in motion. In loglines, it is often more effective to omit the characters' names. Instead, well-chosen adjectives can give the reader a wealth of information about a character.

Loglines are most effective when they are built around a goal. This is not only about the protagonist, but also about the protagonist's motivation. The goal should explain the story and perhaps even name the conflict. It should be clearly formulated without - and this is the difficulty - revealing too much or too little.

For example, a logline might read, "In a dystopian future where water is the most valuable commodity, a young female engineer must find a lost spring." Here, the goal is clearly defined, but there is still a lack of motivation or threat in case the character does not reach her goal.

It's also important to mention the urgency of the goal in the logline. "In a dystopian future where water is the most precious commodity, a young engineer must find a lost spring before her city dies of thirst."

The survival of their town and its people is at stake here,

which makes the pressure and motivation of the characters clear. But the conflict is still not really clear. That's why it makes sense to integrate this element as well:

"In a dystopian future where water is the most precious commodity, a young engineer must find a lost spring before her city dies of thirst. But in the process, she discovers a dark secret that the powers that be will protect at all costs."

A logline should convey the main concept of the story without giving away the ending. This way, the reader gets the opportunity to eagerly receive the entire script and still discover something new.

Due to their clear structure, loglines can be generated very well by the AI. A well-trained AI can analyze thousands of these short summaries and recognize patterns in them. With this database, it can then generate its own suggestions that are both creative and in line with the market.

If an author is at the beginning of a project and is looking for a sparkling idea, she can have the AI suggest a number of loglines - on specific topics, genres, or characters. These suggestions can then serve as a starting point for a story.

Above all, however, authors can also ask the AI to make suggestions for loglines at any time during the writing process. For example, all that is needed is to enter the synopsis and ask the AI to present one or more loglines. The AI analyzes the context and the main elements of the story and generates concise and precise loglines as a result. This not only speeds up the process, but also provides different perspectives and wording that might not have occurred to the author.

If an author already has a logline, he or she can enter it into the AI and receive suggestions for improvements or variations. The AI can also estimate whether the summary will be successful on the market.

5.9. Synopses

In the development of stories, the synopsis is an important tool and often a necessary evil. It summarizes the core of a narrative and gives potential broadcasters, producers or publishers a quick overview of the work.

Often, authors are asked to provide a brief summary of the content of about one page. But writing a concise and compelling synopsis can be a challenge. Again, AI can assist authors by scanning a text and identifying the main events, characters, and conflicts. It selects the most important information and ideas from the original text and restates them in a shorter form. Within the AI, there is a mechanism that allows the model to weight the importance of each word in terms of the entire text. This helps the AI to emphasize relevant information and ignore less important details. During the generation process, the model continuously reviews and adjusts its answers to ensure that the summary is coherent and representative of the original text.

As with the logline, it makes sense to enter the original text and ask the AI to generate a short version.

It is helpful to specify the desired length. The AI can even match the style and tone of the synopsis to that of the original work to ensure consistency.

```
Please generate a synopsis for a feature film.
The summary should be 300 words. This is the
text you should summarize: [synopsis].
```

Often, the AI even invents a title (without explicit

prompting) and adds a paragraph at the end that pithily emphasizes the story's specifics.

As in all application areas, it is helpful to take full advantage of AI. This is because the system learns through feedback. If authors are not satisfied with a generated suggestion, they can provide feedback to make the result better. The AI complies with the request to make another suggestion with this feedback without grumbling.

5.10. Title

AI can also helpauthors find titles for films and novels. Finding a title is a unique creative process that varies from author to author, but also from time to time. Once in a while, an author has an inspiration relatively early in the writing process; other times, they have to search for a suitable title for a very long time. Both experiences most authors will have had in the course of their careers. They show how complex the creative process is.

Finding a suitable title quickly is a liberating experience. But there are screenplays and novels where the authors don't have a spontaneous inspiration. They then have to experiment with different ideas, develop suggestions and possibly make several attempts before they feel they have found the right one.

One way is to discuss it with other creative minds, whether friends, colleagues, or even test readers. This brainstorming can generate new ideas and help with decision-making. Sometimes writers or screenwriters take a stack of index cards with individual words and arrange them in different combinations until they find the title that best fits their vision.

A popular approach is to select a key scene or symbol from the script or novel and base the title on it. This method allows the essence or central theme to be reflected in a concise title. One of the iconic key scenes in the novel and film *The Silence of the Lambs* is the famous episode in which the young FBI agent Clarice Starling tells the notorious serial killer Hannibal Lecter about her experience as a little girl when she failed to save her beloved lambs from death on her uncle's farm (see Chapter 5.5). The title refers to this symbolic scene and reflects the dark atmosphere of the narrative.

Authors also often have a particular motif that runs through their story. They may follow this central theme and try to find an appropriate title that captures the heart of their narrative. *The Pursuit of Happyness* is based on the true story of Chris Gardner, who despite great challenges and setbacks, pursues his dream of building a better life for himself and his son. The title highlights the essential motif of the film, which is the search for happiness and fulfillment in the midst of difficult circumstances.

Some novels and screenplays are named after the main character. If the character is particularly memorable or has a profound meaning, his name is very suitable as a title. The movie *Oppenheimer* is named after the scientist and builder of the first atomic bomb, J. Robert Oppenheimer. In rarer cases, another figure is also given a title. These films work with a so-called "central character" who pushes himself into the foreground next to the protagonist. This dramaturgical device is usually used when the author wants to describe either a genius or a person with whom the viewer finds it difficult to identify, but who is often the actual narrative occasion. *Amadeus* and *The Great Gatsby* are examples of films in which the so-called central character is the titular character.

Individual words or phrases from the dialogue of the novel or screenplay can also serve as potential titles. If a particular quote or phrase stands out, it can become an appropriate title. The movie *I am Legend* is about the last surviving human on Earth who fights mutant creatures in a post-apocalyptic world. The 2007 film starring Will Smith is based on the 1954 novel of the same name by Richard Matheson, and the phrase "I am legend" appears in the novel at a key moment. Towards the end of the novel, the protagonist realizes that he himself has become a legend and a monster in the new society dominated by the vampire-like creatures. He is the last of his kind and is feared and despised by the new beings. In this moment of self-knowledge, he accepts his role and place in the new world order. The phrase "I am legend" sums up this realization and equally the irony and tragedy of his situation. It is a moment of reflection that brings together the novel's complex themes of identity, morality, and society.

The use of AI has now made it easier to find a suitable and successful title. Authors can enter the treatment or a longer synopsis (or, if technically possible, the entire work) and have a list of any number of suggestions generated. It can be helpful to consider certain genre-specific conventions. For this reason, the prompt can also explicitly ask for a title that fits the genre.

```
You are a writer and you are looking for a
title for your novel (movie). Generate a list
```

of 5 suggestions for this material. It is a
thriller: [synopsis or treatment].

Again, it may be helpful to inquire further.

I like 2 and 4 from the list. Create another 5
suggestions based on this.

One of the simplest but most effective approaches to how AI can help generate titles is to have it search for known patterns or stylistic elements in a list of existing titles. The AI analyzes these titles and captures the structural and semantic features to derive new combinations and variations.

While content descriptions can provide a broad base of inspiration, targeted prompts are a powerful tool for directing the AI to specific features, moods, or themes. Authors can use directed prompts to describe the context or desired atmosphere of the novel or movie, and the AI can then generate titles that fit those specifications exactly.

For example, an author wants to find a title for a road movie in which two sisters travel to visit their terminally ill father in San Fransisco. The directed prompt might read:

Generate 5 titles for a feature film with the
following content: "Journey by car through
America to San Francisco, on which the two
hostile sisters become close again." The title
should suggest a light comedy.

As a result, the AI can generate a variety of titles that match that description exactly, even though they may not quite fit yet:

1. "Sisters on the 101: A Highway to Harmony"
2. "Frisco Bound: Steering Through Sisterhood"
3. "The Golden Gate Getaway: A Sisterly

Reunion"
4. "Coast to Coast with Sisterly Ghosts"
5. "Bridging Sisters: A Road Trip to Remember"

These directed prompts help focus on specific aspects and allow authors to target appropriate titles without getting lost in endless brainstorming sessions.

Finding the perfect title is an important creative decision. Authors should make intensive use of AI to find the title that captures the essence of their story and piques the interest of readers and potential producers.

Although AI can be a valuable aid in finding titles, it is essential to emphasize thatauthors still play the decisive role. The titles generated serve as a source of inspiration and pave the way for new ideas, which are then further developed by the creatives.

AI technology continues to evolve, and it is foreseeable that the areas of application will become increasingly diverse. In the future, AI systems could generate even more complex titles that not only reflect the structure and theme of the work, but also take into account the emotional response of the target audience.

But the titles of the screenplay or novel manuscript are not always identical to the later title on the screen or cover. The titles suggested by the authors serve as an internal reference for the publishers, the production team, the marketing team and the editors. Here, it serves to clarify the content direction and the core of the story. But once the process of filming or publishing begins, other considerations gain weight.

Titles must not only capture the essence of the plot, but also appeal to the audience and arouse their curiosity. Here, marketing and accessibility play a crucial role. A working title that accurately reflects the plot but has little emotional appeal will not capture the interest of potential readers and viewers. Publishers and distributors therefore often look for their own titles to achieve greater reach and make the work more attractive.

The more an author already takes these aspects into consideration, the higher the probability that her title will endure.

For this purpose, it can assign the role of a marketer to the AI and have the title verified (see Chapter 6.9). In this way, the AI also conducts quick and efficient market research by checking how potential viewers react to different titles. This could also help, at least in part, to better assess the success of a film or series even before its release.

5.11. Scenes and the art of creating dialog

The creation of AI-generated scenes and dialog is a milestone in the development of creative technologies. Early attempts were limited to predictable and often clunky formulations that had limited utility for authors (see also *Sunspring* in Chapter 3.3). However, with the advancement of Deep Learning and natural language processing (NLP), the quality and versatility of AI-generated dialogues has improved significantly. AI models now have the ability to produce human-like text that is extremely convincing in grammar, style, and even atmosphere. This opens up whole new possibilities for authors looking for inspiration, inspiration, and new perspectives.

Currently, however, it is not yet the case that a single prompt enables the AI to create a scene that approximates human invention. Rather, it is a process with several stages on which the AI generates helpful suggestions.

Creating a compelling scene starts with a clear idea and conceptualization. Before using AI, it's critical to thoroughly understand the scenario, character dynamics, and emotional resonance of the scene. This requires time to outline the basics, including relationships between characters, the overall tone of the scene, and key moments to highlight.

Even at this stage, the AI can be asked to provide inspiration. For example, an author can work with the AI to examine the dynamics of a scene or think about the posture of characters. A question for this could be like this:

```
Can you put yourself in Ashley's shoes? What
will Ashley think when she meets Dr. Thompson
there?
```

The AI is also useful for detailed descriptions, whether for places, objects or people. At the push of a button, the AI can provide variations and suggested wording for all types of descriptions, from which the author can then choose.

A crucial role for a scene (especially in a movie) is the location. Often authors give away the chance for a dynamic scene because they have chosen a wrong location. Again, the AI can provide a list of alternatives. It is helpful to enter the parameters of the scene and have a selection of ideas suggested. The AI can be fed with the atmosphere or the desired emotional effect of a scene. Possibly, the completed scene can be uploaded into the system, which can then suggest an interesting and exciting location. With this new location, the author can then rewrite the scene.

After a solid foundation for the scene is established, the AI can be used more concretely. Clear instructions about the characters, context, and tone of voice make it possible to elicit specific, appropriate suggestions from the AI. For example, if a character in the story is particularly sarcastic, this should be communicated to the AI so that its dialogue reflects that aspect of the personality.

> Write a complete scene with dialogue and stage directions. Start with the scene title. The scene is based on the following information: [Information].

Another application for the AI is writing from other perspectives. If the author wants to change the point of view in a scene, he can feed the AI with the character profiles and the previous action and then have it draft the scene from the point of view of an alternative character. This can provide new insights and enrich the work.

Dialogues are the heart of every scene. They not only carry information and plot lines, but also convey the emotions, relationships and conflicts between the characters.

Often the first drafts from the AI are banal suggestions with sentences like those very often found in soap operas. These so-called soap operas are known for their dramatic, emotionally charged and sometimes exaggerated dialogues. The conversations between the characters are usually characterized by intense emotions, secrets and intrigue. They are often predictable and characterized by melodramatic flair. Thus, the AI also tends towards this form of conversation. This is where the author's fine-tuning begins. For example, it might be important to give the scene and its dialogues more subtext. That's why it's beneficial to feed the concept behind subtext into the system. This is very easy and it is a good idea to let the AI do the work.

```
Do you know the concept of subtext in scenes?
```

The AI will (most likely) reply that it knows the concept and explain it right away. Now the AI can be instructed to rewrite the scene again, using more subtext. This involves copying the definition that the AI itself gave into the prompt once again, so that the concept is really present.

```
Please rewrite completely. Dialogue should be
with a lot of subtext. Subtext refers to the
unspoken or less obvious meanings or emotions
behind a character's actual words. It is what
is read between the lines and is often
conveyed through body language, tone of voice,
facial expressions, and other nonverbal cues.
```

The AI will write a new draft that is closer to the desired result.

5.12. Acoustic mask

Every character should have a unique voice that reflects their personality. The writer and Nobel Prize winner for literature Elias Canetti coined the term "acoustic mask" for this.

Each person uses his own vocabulary and a structure of his sentences. Canetti emphasizes that this is something singular that belongs only to that person. It is similar with the characters in novels and screenplays. They, too, should have a specific acoustic mask that distinguishes them from the other characters.

The AI can be used to try out different speaking styles for different characters. Thus, the AI can be fed with the most important parameters of a character. It is then asked to write a text in the language of that character. And the system can even be asked to rewrite already existing dialogs according to the acoustic mask of the respective character.

5.13. Status

A helpful point for a dialogue can be the question about the respective status of the characters. The renowned British theater maker Keith Johnstone has emphasized in his book *Impro: Improvisation and the Theatre* that the dynamics of any conversation are strongly influenced by the status of the interlocutors. For Johnstone, the focus is less on social status and more on the position a character occupies in relation to his or her counterpart. A character can be socially low status but still exude high status, and vice versa.

Throughout life, everyone develops a certain ability to adopt a particular status that provides them with security. According to Johnstone, everyone becomes a "master of status," with some people embodying a particular status better than others. The main goal of any conversation, whether conscious or unconscious, is to achieve or maintain a certain status. Status is therefore not rigid, but can change in the course of a communication. Importantly, characters either seek to elevate or demean themselves by ascribing the opposite status to their counterpart.

In any dialogue in a novel or screenplay, there is an underlying status dynamic. Even the most neutral comments can be seen as indicators of the speaker's status position. A real-life relationship works best when one partner assumes the lower status and the other the higher status. However, it becomes especially exciting in fiction when both aspire to the same status or when the status assumed is at odds with social norms. Dialogue becomes more lively when characters compete for the same status, even if they get along well on the outside.

Here, too, the AI can support the author. Some dialogs do not develop enough dynamics because the status question is not designed in an interesting way. The author can ask the AI to rewrite a dialog with a different status situation. In this way, it is very quickly apparent whether a rewrite is appealing in this sense.

Here's how the AI can paraphrase the following (non-award winning) dialogue between a nurse and her head doctor:

Dr. Reynolds: Jane, please come in and sit down.

Jane: Yes, Dr. Reynolds. Sorry for the inconvenience.

Dr. Reynolds: It's about the incident with Mr. Knauer last night. He received the wrong dose of medication. How could that have happened?

Jane: I ... I'm really very sorry, Dr. Reynolds. I ... I don't know how I could have missed that.

Dr. Reynolds: Jane, such mistakes are unacceptable. We have a responsibility here, and such negligence can cost a patient's life.

Jane: I understand, Dr. Reynolds. It was a long day and I was tired, but that's no excuse. I ... I really don't know what to say.

Dr. Reynolds: Fatigue is no excuse, Jane. You must always be on top of your tasks. What if Mr. Knauer had serious complications now?

Jane: I can't imagine how terrible that would be. I am really deeply affected and regret my mistake. I will do everything so that something like this never happens again.

Dr. Reynolds: I expect the same from you. You will attend additional training and I will make sure that you are closely monitored until I am sure that such a mistake will not happen again.

Jane: Yes, Dr. Reynolds. I will do anything you ask. I really want you to know how sorry I am.

Dr. Reynolds: Your remorse is noted, Jane. But I expect action, not words. You can go now.

Jane: Yes, Dr. Reynolds. Thank you for taking the time to talk to me. I will do better. I promise that.

Again, it is useful to first ask the AI if it knows the concept of high and low status. When the system has satisfactorily explained this question, the author can give it the task of rewriting the scene.

```
Rewrite the dialogue. Jane has the high status
and Reynolds has the low status [Dialogue
scene].
```

The alternative AI proposal is:

Jane: Dr. Reynolds, I heard you wanted to talk to me?

Dr. Reynolds: Um, yes, Jane. It's about the incident with Mr. Knauer last night. It seems that he received the wrong dose of medication. I ... I'm not sure how that could have happened.

Jane: Dr. Reynolds, I am aware of the problem. It was my mistake, and I take full responsibility for it. But I would like to emphasize that despite this mistake, I take my duties here very seriously.

Dr. Reynolds: I ... I understand, Jane. But such mistakes can have serious consequences. How could this happen?

Jane: It was a long and hectic day, Dr. Reynolds. But that's no excuse. I've already taken steps to make sure this doesn't happen in the future. I expect the highest standard from myself, and I will make sure that I meet that standard in the future.

Dr. Reynolds: I appreciate your honesty and commitment, Jane. But we have to make sure that such mistakes are avoided.

Jane: I understand that, Dr. Reynolds. And I will do everything I can to regain the trust you have placed in me. I have already spoken to the pharmacist and planned additional training. I will not allow anything like this to happen again.

Dr. Reynolds: Thank you, Jane. I hope that we can avoid such incidents in the future. I trust that you will take the necessary steps.

Jane: You can count on me, Dr. Reynolds. It won't happen again.

Of course, the respective status must fit the characters. But there can also be scenes with characters that appear only once or twice. Very quickly, the AI can write these conversations with a different constellation and the author can decide whether this variant is more interesting.

The dialog generated by the AI is a starting point, not a final product. It is the author's job to revise, refine and adapt the text to the overall flow of the scene. In this way, human nuances, emotions and individual voices are added to make the dialogs come alive.

Overall, it is important to maintain the authenticity of the characters and the plot. Although the AI can generate amazingly realistic sentences, it is up to the author to ensure that the generated dialogs are not only grammatically correct, but also fit the personality of the characters and the context of the story. If a dialogue doesn't seem quite coherent, adjustments should be made to maintain authenticity.

Especially in the dialogue scenes, it becomes clear once again that the ethical limitations of AI are rather a disadvantage in this case. Most large AI models like GPT-3 were explicitly trained not to use obscene, violent, or stereotypical language. This was done for good reasons, to avoid the spread of harmful content. For authors, however, this means that the AI often generates tame and well-behaved dialogue suggestions that contain little potential for conflict or drama. They tend to be harmless, predictable conversations that fall within social norms.

To put it metaphorically: The AI assistants for dialog generation actually behave like well-behaved nuns who don't want to subject anyone to overly coarse or provocative formulations. They hold back and avoid any risk.

For authors, this can be a hindrance, as dialogues are often meant to be full of emotion, provocation and drastic language in order to achieve an intense effect. Of course, artists also want their characters to curse, argue, or threaten in order to write authentic, gripping scenes.

This is indeed where the limits of the AI become apparent. In order to use the full potential for powerful dialogs, narrators must manually give the AI more freedom and specifically feed it with examples. Otherwise, dialogue suggestions will remain too boring and sterile. AI ethics and exciting dialogs can only be reconciled through conscious human intervention.

5.14. Transitioning from Page to Screen

Adapting a novel into a screenplay is an art in itself. It's a process that requires both respect for the original source and a deep understanding of the unique requirements of the film medium. While a novel can get lost in the thoughts and feelings of its characters, a script usually needs to be more concrete and action-oriented in order to visually and emotionally engage the audience.

The first step in this process is to read the novel closely. This involves not only understanding the plot, but also capturing the tone, atmosphere, and deeper themes of the book. This helps the screenwriter identify the core of the story and decide which elements are most important for the cinematic adaptation.

Now the adaptation process can begin. Screenwriters' approaches to this work can vary widely and are often as individual as the writers themselves. Some screenwriters read the novel only once to get a feel for the story, characters, and atmosphere. They then rely on that fresh first impression to translate the essence of the book into a screenplay. The one-time run-through helps them focus on the most important elements of the story, and not get lost in the details. This approach can be especially useful when the screenwriter is trying to offer an unusual interpretation or a new angle on the narrative.

On the other hand, there are screenwriters who have the novel constantly at hand as they write the script. They create detailed annotations, underline key scenes, and return to specific passages again and again to capture the nuances and subtleties of the original. This approach is recommended if the screenwriter wants to remain very faithful to the original work, or if the novel contains complex plot lines and character developments that need to be carefully transferred into the screenplay.

Both approaches have their merits and can be effective depending on the novel and the screenwriter's intentions. The important thing is that the screenwriter finds a method that helps him or her bring the story to the screen authentically and effectively.

Through AI, however, the screenwriter now has support that can make the process more efficient, precise and creative. Of course, the writer's copyright must be observed at all costs. It's easy when the work to be adapted is centuries old and no such rights exist anymore. In the USA, copyrights generally expire 70 years after the author's death. For works published before 1923, they are generally in the public domain because the copyright has expired. This means that they can be used by anyone. (In the case of a remake of *The Scarlet Letter* by Nathaniel Hawthorne or Franz Kafka's *The Trial*, this would be the case). The situation is different if these rights still exist. Then, of course, the work cannot be entered into the AI without the author's permission. But the screenwriter can work with his own prompts.

First, for copyright-free works, AI can be used to analyze the structure and main themes of a novel. Using advanced text analysis algorithms, AI can identify key events, character developments, and thematic patterns in the novel. This information can help screenwriters understand the core of the story and decide which elements are most important for adaptation. Instead of working through hundreds of pages again, the screenwriter can get a detailed analysis of the novel that gives them a clear overview of the story.

A prompt might look like this:

```
Create a list of all the key events in the
novel: [Novel].
```

Generally, the screenwriter first creates a treatment to check how the flow of the narrative can be realized cinematically. This often involves revising the structure of the novel to fit the typical format of a film. While books can often be told at a slower pace, with detailed descriptions and inner monologues, a film usually needs to be tighter and more focused. This means that some scenes must be shortened, altered, or omitted altogether to maintain the flow and momentum of the film. The AI may be asked to distill the core of the plot in free novels. This can provide the author with an outline and give her imagination room to see how the story can be realized.

In addition, for classics, AI can help identify dialogue and scenes that are particularly impactful or emotional. By analyzing speech patterns and context, AI can pick out scenes that are most likely to evoke a strong reaction from the audience. This can help the screenwriter decide which key moments to keep in the adaptation.

```
What scenes in the novel are particularly
impactful or emotional? [Novel]
```

Character development is another key element in the adaptation. While novels often develop their dramatis personae over many pages, a film has to get to the point more quickly. This doesn't mean that character maturation is less important in cinema or television, but that it must be done in a different way: Dialogue, plot and visual cues are the cinematic means to establish the characters quickly and effectively. AI can play a role in this as well. It can identify the interactions and relationships between characters in the novel (when copyrights no longer exist) and create a detailed profile of each character. This makes their motivations, emotions, and developments easier to understand, and the adaptation can become more authentic.

Another central aspect of the adaptation is the consideration of which parts of the novel are visually representable.

> Which scenes in the novel would translate well to a visual medium? [Novel]

The AI not only selects scenes, but also gives hints on how these can be implemented. For example, it writes "This could be filmed well with a handheld camera in a documentary style." Or "This could be shown from several perspectives, also as a slow-motion effect."

An interior monologue that works in the novel may need to be replaced with plot or dialogue in the film. Similarly, complex storylines that run over several chapters in the book may be too confusing in the film and may need to be simplified or shortened. Here, too, AI can be used in a supportive manner. For example, the AI can be asked to suggest how an inner monologue can be translated into action.

There are also practical considerations in adaptation. For example, a novel set in exotic or hard-to-reach locations may be too expensive or logistically complex for a film production. In such cases, the screenwriter must find creative solutions to bring the story into a cinematically viable form. The AI can be asked to suggest alternative locations with the necessary information. The parameters that the new location must fulfill can also be defined. This could look like this:

```
For a novel, I am looking for another place
where the filmed story takes place. The place
should be in Canada and by the sea. It should
have a lively restaurant scene and there
should be a large university with many
students.
```

Dialog is also of great importance. While novels like to indulge in the luxury of extensive conversations, movies have to get to the point faster. A screenwriter can ask the AI how to tighten up a dialog and make it sound natural at the same time.

One advantage of AI is its ability to take cultural and historical contexts into account. When adapting a historical novel or a work set in another culture, the AI can provide relevant information by accessing the screenwriter's extensive databases, making the script historically accurate and authentic.

One interesting facet that AI can help with is predicting audience reaction. By analyzing data on similar films or adaptations, AI can make predictions about how viewers will react to certain scenes, characters, or storylines. These predictions can help the screenwriter maximize the impact of the film.

Overall, AI offers a wealth of possibilities when translating a novel into a screenplay. From analyzing the structure and themes of the original to character development and predicting audience reaction, AI can help the process at every stage. But again, the screenwriter's creative vision and intuition always take center stage, and AI can be a valuable tool that enriches and enhances the adaptation process.

5.15. Conflicts

In the world of stories, conflict is at the heart of every narrative. It is the engine that drives the plot, shapes the characters, and captivates the reader or viewer. Without conflict, there would be no change, no progress, and no development; in short, there would be nothing to tell.

First of all, conflict is a reflection of the human experience. Since the dawn of time, humans have experienced controversy, whether on a personal, social, or global level. These disputes shape our understanding of good and evil, right and wrong. Storytellers who narrate conflicts therefore address universal truths that are deeply rooted in the collective psyche.

Last but not least, the conflict serves to create tension and interest. A smooth narrative flow in which everything goes according to plan may be pleasant, but it quickly becomes boring; it is not worth telling. Confrontation, on the other hand, creates uncertainty, generates questions, and keeps the reader or viewer engaged. Conflict forces the audience to wonder, "What will happen next? How will the character react? How will the situation resolve?" This curiosity is what keeps readers turning page after page or keeps viewers tuned in until the end of the film or series.

In addition, conflict allows for character development. Through challenges and adversity, the characters are tested, their weaknesses exposed, and their strengths highlighted. A protagonist who does not experience confrontation remains static and one-dimensional. It is the conflict that gives her depth, nuance and credibility. It forces the character to decide, to act and to grow.

Therefore, a decisive task for AI would be to work with conflicts and to bring them to a head if possible.

However, this is exactly where the AI fails in the first moment.

While authors consider conflicts as part of their activity, AI tends to avoid or overlook them. First, it is important to understand that AI systems are designed in their basic structure to recognize patterns and find solutions to given problems. They are not programmed to know the nuances and complexities of human emotions and relationships. So when an AI is faced with a conflict, it tries to develop the "most efficient" way to resolve the disturbance without considering the deeper emotional and social aspects. This can lead to decisions that seem superficial.

In addition, AI systems are usually designed to minimize risks. Conflicts are often seen as risk factors to be avoided. But forauthors, tension is not a bad thing; it is the DNA of their novels or screenplays. By avoiding conflict, AI misses out on the opportunity to tell good and exciting stories. Because AI tends to prevent or quickly resolve controversies, it robs the narrative of its depth and complexity. Instead of drawing the reader or viewer into a sustained emotional experience, it delivers a flat, predictable narrative that leaves little room for tension or empathy.

But this initial reaction of the AI can be overcome and worked on by creatives. Again, it helps to think of the model as a co-author who is known to be conflict averse. So the model must be decidedly invited to allow conflicts and to invent them.

After the prompt to the AI to write a story of an astronaut who wants to return to Earth, the system invents the story of Alex, whose spaceship has been damaged by a meteor shower and whose communication to Earth has been interrupted.

> Days turned into weeks and weeks into months. Without contact with Earth, Alex felt lonely and isolated. His supplies were dwindling, and the hope of ever returning home seemed increasingly unlikely. But in his despair, he remembered an old legend he had heard as a child: of a mysterious stargate that could guide travelers through space and time.
>
> With this hope in his heart, Alex did everything he could to find this stargate. He studied old star charts and followed the clues he found in the depths of space. After months of searching, he finally came across a glowing portal that shimmered in the darkness of space.

In fact, the AI resolves obstacles very quickly and finds ways to bring the narrative to a positive end swiftly. Without going deeper into Alex's difficulties, it conjures up a solution. The search for the stargate also proceeds without any real confrontation.

Therefore, the author should rather ask the AI right at the beginning if it is familiar with the concept of conflicts in stories. This serves to make the AI aware of the phenomenon of confrontation. The AI is then asked to invent a section of the narrative that is full of conflict and tension.

Days turned into weeks and weeks into months. Without contact with the earth, Alex felt lonely and isolated. Every day was a battle against the rising despair and dwindling oxygen. His supplies dwindled, and hopes of ever returning home seemed increasingly futile. One day, when he was about to lose heart, he discovered an old diary on board that had come from his grandfather, one of the first space travelers of his time.

In this diary, he read about an old legend he had heard as a child: about a mysterious stargate that could take travelers through space and time. But the gate was guarded by a dangerous creature that destroyed anyone who tried to pass through it. With renewed courage and determination, Alex set out to find this gate, determined to risk everything to return home.

His journey took him through black holes, past exploding stars and through dangerous asteroid fields. Finally, he found the stargate, but as the legend had predicted, it was guarded by the fearsome creature. In an epic battle, in which Alex had to use all his knowledge and skills, he finally managed to defeat the creature and pass through the stargate. When he came out on the other side, he found himself in orbit around Earth, ready to tell his incredible story.

The obedient AI has fulfilled the mission and at least integrated rudiments of antagonistic forces into the search for the stargate.

The AI tends to suggest general and known solutions the first time. But as we have seen, this can be refined.

It is helpful to pick up one aspect of the proposal and work on it. Unlike a human co-author, the AI is also not touchy and certainly not miffed.

```
The idea of the scary creature is a cliché.
Can you think of something more original?
```

The AI also picks up on this prompt and offers an alternative solution:

```
Of course, I understand your point. Let's frame
the conflict differently:
Days turned into weeks and weeks into months.
Without contact with Earth, Alex felt lonely and
isolated. His supplies were dwindling, and the
hope of ever returning home seemed more and
more futile. One day, he stumbled across an old
record on board from the ship's first crew.
The record spoke of a stargate guarded not by
monsters or creatures, but by a riddle that could
be solved only with the combined memories and
experiences of all the astronauts who had ever
traveled space. The gate would be accessible only
to those who understood the essence of humanity
and its relationship to the cosmos.
Alex began searching the ship's databases,
reading astronauts' diaries, listening to their
music, seeing their art, and trying to understand
the common bond they all shared. He meditated,
dreamed, and reflected on his own experiences in
space.
```

After weeks of intense searching and self-reflection, Alex believed he had found the answer. He approached the stargate and was confronted by a holographic interface that asked him to solve the riddle of humanity. With deep breath and firm belief in his findings, he entered his answer.
The stargate shone brightly and opened, and Alex found himself in orbit around Earth. Not only had he solved the riddle of the stargate, but he had discovered a deeper connection to himself and to humanity as a whole.

The prompt was kept very general. It would be quite possible to specify further parameters here. Thus, approaches for solutions could be offered or even references to other narratives could be given.

Once again, this response highlights the AI's tendency to provide every conflict and story with a fairy tale ending. It is surprising that the AI does not provide all suggestions with a "And they lived happily ever after".

If authors want to generate their creations with a less positive or even tragic ending, they can explicitly request this. If a story is desired that ends with an unresolved conflict, this should be specified in the request. For example, "Tell this story so that it ends with an unresolved conflict."

After a proposal is generated by the AI, and the characters ride off into the sunset together, alternative conclusions can be asked for that are less positive or even negative.

If authors are not yet satisfied with the proposals, they should communicate this. Feedback helps the AI to better understand the requirements and respond accordingly.

Emotional cues such as "tragic," "heartbreaking," or "conflicted" can be used in the assignment to the AI to mark the desired mood.

5.16. Humor

When asked for a joke, the AI responds:

> Why can't ghosts tell lies?
> Because you can see through them!

Well, yes, but in the field of AI, humor has always been considered a complex and elusive area. AI has made significant progress in several fields, from solving challenging games like Go and chess to generating coherent text. However, its understanding of humor is not yet mature. The nature of comedy, which is deeply rooted in human experience, cultural nuances, and social conventions, presents a unique challenge for machines.

Early attempts to make AI models humorous were rather disappointing. Early systems often gave literal or overly technical answers that completely missed the human sense of irony or sarcasm. For example, when asked "Why did the chicken cross the road?" the system replied, "I'm a computer program and don't understand the context of jokes." Technically correct, but far from humorous.

Tony Veale, professor at University College Dublin, points out that humor is a fundamental human trait. Understanding a person's sense of wit gives insight into their personality and worldview. Unlike games with set rules, comedy is often about breaking social conventions and norms. For a machine to be humorous, it must recognize which standards it can break and when.

The AI's response to the prompt to create a Ricky Gervais-style joke about the AI was parried as follows.

> "You know, I read that AI is now writing poetry,
> composing music, and even making art. That's
> great, isn't it? Finally, someone to blame for all the
> terrible pop songs on the radio. 'Oh, that new
> number one hit? Yeah, it's not a human's fault this
> time, it's AI!' And when it's a hit, who gets the
> royalty check? Does it go to the AI? Maybe they
> spend it on electric bills and software updates.
> 'Sorry, love, can't go out tonight, I've got to
> update my antivirus. It's a real party in my
> circuits!'"

Veale believes that as AI models evolve, they will develop components that are essential to humor, such as a sense of incongruity. Current systems already show abilities to detect discrepancies, suggesting that they are gradually laying the groundwork for a more refined sense of humor. The challenge is to move from simply detecting absurdities to turning them into genuinely funny content.

And humor is a deeply human phenomenon, often shaped by cultural, social, and individual nuances. A joke that is funny in one culture may be misunderstood or perceived as offensive in another.

But Veale may not be wrong in his assessment. Because there is indeed progress, too. Newer AI models trained on massive amounts of data have begun to show a rudimentary understanding of humor. They can recognize simple jokes and even generate some humorous responses.

6. AI as a partner

AI not only helps authors with the pure writing of a story, but is also a great support when it comes to thinking outside the box, offering alternative perspectives, breaking down entrenched thought patterns and promoting innovative ideas. To do this, it takes on a variety of roles, ranging from acting as an advisor, a feedback-giver, to a co-author actively involved in shaping storylines or character development. The ability of AI to take on such roles expands the boundaries of what is possible in creative work.

6.1. The kind and patient co-author

While many writers work alone, teamwork has led to some of the most successful scripts and important iconic films. Although these partnerships are rare in literature, the idea that two heads are better than one has a long tradition in the film industry. Screenwriting teams are often able to combine their different skills and perspectives to develop complex and multi-layered stories. Within such partnerships, writers have often succeeded in challenging each other, overcoming creative blocks, and writing scripts that might not have been possible on their own.

In literature, French authors Pierre Boileau and Thomas Narcejac have successfully collaborated for years. The author duo is known for its crime novels, on the basis of which various films were made. In 1954, for example, the novel *D'entre les morts* appeared, which served as a template for Alfred Hitchcock's *Vertigo*.

A notable example of a highly prolific pair of screenwriters is the collaboration between Joel and Ethan Coen. The Coen brothers have created a unique style and tone with films like *The Big Lebowski*, No *Country for Old Men*, and *Fargo*. Their creative synergy has resulted not only in impressive screenplays, but multi-layered characters and unforgettable dialogue.

Another legendary partnership was that between Billy Wilder and I.A.L. Diamond. Together they created timeless classics such as *Some Like It Hot*, *The Apartment* and *Sunset Boulevard*, which featured sharp dialogue, intelligent storylines and subtle satire and had a decisive impact on Hollywood's Golden Age.

Of course, the cooperation of teams of authors also brings its own challenges. Creative differences can arise, and finding a common artistic tone often requires compromise. But it's precisely these difficulties that can lead to an even deeper engagement with the story and characters, and in the best cases, result in a stronger novel or screenplay.

A key benefit of writing teams is the ability to work on different aspects of a story simultaneously. While one is honing a theme, the other can be working on another scene or developing plot ideas. This often speeds up the writing process and encourages continued story development. Also, in the best cases, the different skills on the team complement each other. While one is more apt to design the structure, the other may be able to exercise her strength in writing scenes.

In the future, the use of AI as a co-author is possible. A professional writer with years of experience in the industry may initially wonder how a machine can ever capture the creativity and nuances of human creation. But the relationship between an author and AI can be much more complex than it first appears. In fact, AI can serve as a kind of "friend" to whom the author can turn for inspiration, advice, and ideas.

The idea of using an AI as a creative partner may still sound futuristic to some, but experience shows that this is no longer a utopian scenario. Let's imagine an author sitting at his desk to work on his latest project. He has a clear vision of the plot and characters, but he has an important decision to make regarding the story. Instead of spending hours poring over every detail, he might just ask his AI co-writer. He gives the AI some basic information about the plot and characters and asks for clues about his choices. Within seconds, the AI provides an assessment of the consequences in each case.

```
You are my professional co-author. Here is our
story [story]. We have to decide [question].
What is your assessment?
```

Mostly, the AI now lists the effects of all possibilities. And of course the author still has to and can make the decision himself, but he may have avoided hours of pondering. This example in particular shows what the strengths of the AI are. Just like with a co-author, the author can clarify many things in a dialog. The point is not just to get a question answered, but to keep asking. The AI remembers (differently well depending on the version of the AI) what has already been discussed and can thus conduct a human-like conversation.

Authors read their versions again and again, and sometimes they realize that a solution they have found in the story is not yet satisfactory. If the muse is having a good day, she'll have a better alternative ready. But sometimes that's not the case, and creatives want a co-author they can quickly ask for a better idea. With AI, this sparring partner is now available, whom authors can ask again and again if they can't think of anything useful themselves.

```
Name 3 ways to solve [problem]. I came up with
this [own solution]. But this seems to me too
[criticism].
```

The idea of considering AI as a "friend" or creative partner can seem a bit alienating at first. After all, writing a screenplay or a novel is a highly personal process that often reflects deep emotions and thoughts of the artist. But this view neglects the fact that AI does not serve as a substitute for human imagination, but as a tool that extends and enhances that creativity.

One notable benefit of working with AI is the speed with which ideas can be generated. A writer can save valuable time by asking the AI for quick ideas for scenes, conflicts, or twists that inspire and help them along. This is especially useful when there are tight deadlines to meet and pressure on creative productivity.

Every author has certain thought patterns and blind spots. AI can also deal with this deficit and provide new ideas.

6.2. Sentiment analysis

In literature and film, emotions are elemental to any story. They create a connection between the protagonists and drive the plot forward. To ensure that the words also evoke the desired emotions, emotional text analysis, a special application area of AI, can be used.

This evaluation, often referred to as sentiment analysis, is a process in which AI models identify and categorize the emotional content of a text. By training with large amounts of text data tagged with emotional tags, the AI learns to recognize patterns and relationships between words and emotions. Upon input, the AI analyzes the text and assigns an emotion to each paragraph or sentence. This provides the author with objective feedback on how a work might resonate with an audience, i.e., whether certain passages or chapters will have the intended effect.

If this is not the case, the AI also offers the opportunity for revision here.

```
Please analyze the following text for
emotional content and return an overview of
the predominant emotions in each section:
[text].
```

After the author inserts her text or script, the AI will analyze what she has written and provide detailed feedback about the emotions detected in each paragraph or sentence. This could take the form of tags such as "joy," "sadness," "anger," etc., depending on the emotions identified in the text.

In this way, sentiment analysis can offer deeper insights into specific aspects of the work. For example, an author has the opportunity to check whether chapters or scenes involving specific characters or storylines elicit particularly positive or negative reactions. This allows him to better understand which elements of his writing resonate most and which may need revision.

6.3. SWOT analysis

An important planning tool that helps companies identify their strengths and weaknesses and make strategic decisions is the so-called SWOT analysis. However, this tool can also be used very well in the creative field.

SWOT stands for Strengths, Weaknesses, Opportunities and Threats. The method helps to get a comprehensive picture of a situation or a problem. By analyzing these four aspects, new ideas and solutions can be found.

Strengths	Weaknesses
Opportunities	Threats

The SWOT analysis consists of four main components:

1. strengths (Strengths): This part of the analysis focuses on internal positives. Here, the unique advantages and resources that differentiate a project from others are identified. These could be innovative ideas, time and resources, or passion and commitment.

2. weaknesses (Weaknesses): This section identifies internal challenges and weaknesses. These can be limited resources, creative blocks, or lack of inspiration. Identifying weaknesses enables authors to work on improvement measures.

3. opportunities: Here, external factors that are favorable to

the project should be explored. Opportunities could arise from market trends, changing exploiters, or new technologies. Authors should take advantage of these opportunities to promote their projects.

4. threats: This aspect deals with external risks and obstacles that could affect the project. These could be lack of acceptance, competition or communication problems. The identification of threats helps to develop strategies.

The actual SWOT analysis is performed by creating a matrix in which strengths and weaknesses are assigned to internal factors, while opportunities and threats are external factors. The analysis requires an honest and objective assessment of each aspect.

Authors can use AI to develop a SWOT analysis for their project. Here, too, it is useful to ask the system in advance whether it knows the method, and then to prompt in this way:

```
Can you give me a SWOT analysis of this
project: [text]?
```

Again, the story of Ashley's nightmares is used.

Strengths (Strengths):
-Unique premise: The idea of blurring the lines between dreams and reality is intriguing and could appeal to a wide audience.
-Psychological Depth: The film provides an opportunity to explore complex psychological themes of trauma, memory, and reality.
-Suspense elements: The elements of the psychological thriller can provide high tension and unexpected twists.

-Character development: The main character Ashley offers a lot of room for character development and emotional depth.

Weaknesses:

-Complexity: The merging of dream and reality could be confusing for the audience if not executed well.

-Risk of stereotyping: portrayal of mental health problems must be sensitive and well researched to avoid stereotyping and stigmatization.

-Budget: Depending on the implementation, special effects for dream sequences could be expensive.

-Audience Limitation: The film may be less appealing to younger audiences or people who don't like thrillers.

Opportunities:

-Cult potential: Well realized, the film could achieve cult status and gain a loyal fan base.

-Merchandising: opportunities for books, games, or other ancillary products that expand the world of film.

-Festival Success: The film could do well at film festivals because of its uniqueness and depth.

-streaming services: The rising popularity of streaming services provides an additional platform for distribution.

Threats:

-Competition: There are many psychological thrillers, and the film must stand out clearly to be successful.

-Critical reception: if the film is poorly executed, it could be torn apart by critics, which would hurt its commercial success.
-Sensitive topics: Misrepresenting mental health or trauma could lead to controversy and negative press.
-Time pressure: Trends in film change quickly. If production takes too long, interest in such topics could wane.

After the SWOT analysis is complete, creatives can make strategic decisions. For example, they can leverage the project's strengths, address weaknesses, or develop a targeted strategy to focus on identified opportunities.

6.4. Style

In screenwriting, the focus is on the story and its visual realization, and not necessarily on the author's individual language style. Since film is primarily a visual medium, it is the images, music and acting that set the tone and atmosphere for the audience. The script serves as the foundation for all of these trades, and while it must provide clear visual direction and strong structure, it is not the place for detailed descriptions or introspective prose. Instead, the focus of a script is often on dialogue, which must sound natural and authentic, but should also serve the characters and the plot. It would be fatal, however, if screenwriters tried to impose their own writing style on all their creations.

In the world of literature, an author's individual writing style is often his or her trademark. It is what sets him apart from others and gives him a unique voice. This style, whether through word choice, sentence structure, rhythm, or thematic depth, allows readers to attribute a work to a particular author, much like a brushstroke reveals a painter. A distinctive style can not only give an author recognition and a loyal readership, but also add to the emotional and textual weight of a novel. It adds depth to the narrative, draws the reader into the story, and creates a lasting connection between the work and the reader. Therefore, it is essential for novelists to hone and develop their distinctive style.

AI actually offers the possibility to objectively analyze, understand and refine writing style. Through the use of algorithms and machine learning, it is possible to identify certain patterns, structures, and elements in text that are characteristic of an author's individual style. This technology can not only check grammar and sentence structure, but also evaluate the tone, mood, and coherence of the manuscript. In addition, AI systems can suggest improvements that will make the text more fluid, understandable, or effective. For writers, this is a tool they can use to continuously improve their skills and refine their own style.

The idea of style analysis is not new. For centuries, literary critics and scholars have analyzed authors' writing styles to better understand and interpret their works. But with the advent of AI, the playing field has changed. Instead of relying on subjective interpretations, writers can now use data to gain deeper and objective insights into their novels and manuscripts.

First, the author should have her own style defined - what stylistic devices are used? Are predominantly short, concise sentences used or rather tapeworm sentences? Does the author use poetic language full of metaphors or a sober, functional style? Is the style more humorous-ironic or dramatic-pathetic? The clearer the author's own style profile, the easier it is to develop it.

To analyze one's own writing, the AI can serve as a guide. By submitting passages of text to her, the author can identify stylistic features and provide insights into strengths and weaknesses. The AI's response should also be supported with examples. Otherwise, this should be required in the prompts.

For example, one learns:

> Poetic, figurative language: the text makes use of metaphors ("velvet night") and similes ("like velvet") to create a lyrical mood.

In addition, the AI can present suggestions on how an author can refine or diversify his or her style. Perhaps an author tends to use certain phrases or sentence structures too often. The AI can recognize such patterns and offer more varied or powerful alternatives. Or perhaps the system recognizes that an author is very direct and matter-of-fact in his or her descriptions, and suggests using more metaphorical or imagery-rich language to add more depth and color to the text.

By presenting passages of text to the AI, an author can identify stylistic features and give it insights into his or her strengths and weaknesses.

> Your style is characterized by rich metaphor and expressive adjectives. However, you tend to use a lot of epithets, which inhibits the flow of reading.

Similarly, you can target style exercises to the AI to train certain style facets. The author can ask it, for example:

```
Write this scene again in the style of a
detailed observant realist like Flaubert.
```

The AI then generates text alternatives in the desired style, which the author can rub up against and expand his repertoire. Through such targeted style analyses and experiments under the guidance of the author, the AI becomes a tool that can raise stylistic skills to a higher level.

However, AI is not there to "correct" a writer's style or push them in a particular direction. Rather, it provides a tool for self-reflection, an objective lens through which writers can view their own style. It is then up to the literary person to decide which advice to take and which to ignore.

6.5. Diversity Consulting

In today's world, diversity is more than just a buzzword; diversity is an imperative. Authors of novels and screenplays cannot avoid reflecting diversity in their work. This is not only a matter of social responsibility, but also a means to create stories that are richer, more authentic, and more relevant to a wide audience.

Diversity in literature and film goes beyond the mere representation of different ethnicities or cultures. It includes gender, sexual orientation, socioeconomic status, age, disability, and many other aspects of the human experience. Another important factor of diversity is avoiding stereotypes. Too often, characters are pigeonholed based on their ethnicity, sexual orientation, or other characteristics. This can not only be offensive, but equally detract from the depth and complexity of the characters and the story itself. By avoiding stereotypes and instead creating multi-layered, realistic characters, authors can tell stories that are both compelling and insightful.

There is equally a deeper, cultural value in showing diversity. Stories have the power to shape how we see the world and other people. By incorporating diversity into their works, authors help to reduce prejudice and promote understanding and acceptance of difference. They can also ensure that marginalized groups have a voice and their narratives are heard.

Here, too, AI can be put to good use. It can help authors in various ways to bring more diversity into their characters and stories from the start. The AI can be asked to generate character profiles on different socio-cultural groups:

```
Design the profile of a 45-year-old professor
with Moroccan roots.
```

An author can ask the AI to sketch plot lines from the perspective of underrepresented groups and encourage it to produce dialogue modules between characters of different backgrounds. Or the AI can be asked to generate multiple alternatives to make a character more diverse. The author can engage with these suggestions and enrich his or her writing as a result.

But even after the initial draft, the AI can serve as a watchful eye, detecting and highlighting biases. This allows authors to revise their works for more accurate, respectful representation.

```
Check my text for the portrayal of the
characters. Does the ensemble sufficiently
reflect the reality of life: [text]?
```

But AI goes beyond simply recognizing stereotypes. In an era when data is available at unprecedented levels, AI can provide writers with access to a wealth of information. For example, if a writer wants to write about a particular culture or community, they can use AI to help them provide relevant details, historical context, cultural nuances, and even linguistic subtleties. AI can help make research easier. Instead of spending hours searching for facts or consulting experts, authors can use AI tools to quickly and efficiently access the data they need. This approach can be especially useful when trying to understand historical contexts, research cultural practices, or trace the life experiences of specific communities. But it is precisely here that it is important to note that AI always creates hallucinations and all results need to be verified again (see Chapter 4.3).

Of course, diversity alone is not enough. It's not enough to simply add a character from a particular ethnic group or sexual orientation without really engaging with their experiences and real perspectives. Authenticity is key. Beyond AI interviews, this requires research, empathy, and often consultation with those affected.

There are critics who argue that authors should focus on writing what they know, and that trying to incorporate diversity into their works can seem artificial or forced. While these concerns must be taken seriously, it is equally essential to recognize that creating fiction is always an exercise in empathy. It's about putting yourself in other people's shoes, understanding their experiences, and portraying them in an authentic way. Or to paraphrase Maxim Gorky, "You don't have to have been in a frying pan to write about a schnitzel." With the right research and conscientious approach, authors can incorporate diversity into their stories without it seeming forced or inauthentic.

One of the instruments that has gained some notoriety in recent years is a test for the representation of female characters. The Bechdel test is a simple criterion for evaluating the representation of women in films and other media. A work passes the test if it meets three criteria:

1. there are at least two female characters who are named.

2. these two figures are talking to each other.

3. your conversation is about a topic other than a man.

The test was named after American cartoonist Alison Bechdel, who introduced it in her comic strip *Dykes to Watch Out For* in 1985. It is important to note that the Bechdel test does not necessarily assess the quality or feminism of a film. Instead, it is meant to point out the imbalance in how gender is portrayed in media.

It's hard to believe, but many films, even popular and critically acclaimed ones, fail the Bechdel Test, pointing to a deep-rooted problem in the film industry and in the media landscape as a whole.

It is possible to have the AI check whether a script or novel passes the Bechdel test. In doing so, it is helpful to ask the AI if the system knows the test. Subsequently, the AI is then asked whether the work passes the test.

6.6. The Art of reading a script

In the field of screenwriting, AI can not only serve as a collaborator, but also take on a new role as a script reader. Authors writing their synopsis, treatment, or screenplay are naturally deep in their material, and lack an outside perspective: a fresh and detached look at the work in progress.

AI as a reader can analyze scripts and provide feedback. However, many systems currently have a limitation in terms of the mass of data that the models can process. That's why it's not possible with these providers to upload and edit an entire script (which consists of about 25,000 words). But that's a technical hurdle that very likely won't exist in the next few years. And it's possible for all systems to have treatments or scenes analyzed by the AI. Apart from that, providers already exist today whose limitations exceed several hundred pages (see chap. 7.1).

First of all, script reading by AI means significant time savings. Unlike human consultants, AI can perform analyses at lightning speed and provide rapid feedback. Another key advantage of AI is that it provides objective feedback. It judges and gives advice based on a huge amount of data and complex algorithms. This ensures that the opinion is not clouded by subjective opinions, but is based on solid data and objective criteria.

Nevertheless, it is crucial to emphasize that AI is only a tool and cannot replace the human judgment and intuition of a professional script consultant.

It is helpful for working with the AI to define clear goals for the work on the script. Should character development be optimized, the plot structured, or the dialog improved? By defining their interests, authors can target their assistant.

AI can be applied to many areas of consulting. Here are just a few examples:

1. character analysis and development: The AI can check the consistency of behavior and motivations. It can also suggest how characters can be made deeper to create stronger identification on the part of the audience.

2. plot construction and structure: The AI can analyze the structure of the work to reveal possible weak points in the plot development. It can present suggestions for turning points, conflicts, and climaxes to increase suspense.

3. dialog improvement: the AI can define dialogs that lack depth and emotionality and may be repetitive.

4. target group-oriented adaptation: based on data and genre conventions, the AI can make recommendations for adapting the script to the preferences of the target group.

Here's an example of how authors can ask the AI as a script reader to list the weaknesses of their idea and find ways to improve it:

```
You are an experienced reader of screenplays
with a reputation for meticulous criticism.
Given your experience with refining narrative
structures, character development, and
dramatic elements, how do you evaluate the
proposed story [story]? Consider elements such
as narrative originality, character dynamics,
and potential plot development. Practice
constructive criticism of the premise and
proposed plot.
```

It is also possible to have the AI create a clear table for you:

```
You are a script reader. Analyze the scene
above and list its strengths and weaknesses.
Use a table.
```

On the one hand, the integration of AI into the script consulting process is undoubtedly an advance that can enrich the creative process in many ways. But human script doctors bring a depth of understanding, empathy, and cultural nuance to their analyses that a machine cannot replicate. A text, though written according to certain structures and rules, is at its core a representation of human experience, emotion, and relationships. It therefore requires a human eye and ear to fully grasp and evaluate the subtleties, emotional content, and cultural contexts.

In addition, human consultants have the ability to read between the lines and understand the author's intentions and motivations. They can provide feedback based not only on the text, but also on what the creative may have wanted to express. This is especially important because stories are often informed by the author's deep personal experiences and beliefs.

The use of AI should therefore be considered as a primary step in a broader review and revision process. AI can provide initial analysis, identify structural or thematic problems, and offer innovative suggestions. However, a script doctor should always have the final say to ensure that the story remains or becomes authentic, relevant, and emotionally resonant.

Overall, a combination of AI support and human expertise is the ideal approach. While AI offers speed, efficiency, and objective analysis, the script doctor brings empathy, intuition, and cultural understanding to the process.

Together, the two can help a text reach its full potential and touch an audience in profound ways.

6.7. Breakdown

Writing a screenplay is a complex and often challenging task that requires a deep understanding of story structure and composition. A script is not just a collection of dialogue and instructions, but it is also a carefully constructed work of art made up of various storylines, turning points, and character developments. As you work, it can be easy to lose track of where you are. It's not always obvious at which point a subplot begins, when and where important key moments occur, or when certain characters enter the story.

To meet such challenges and make the script effective, many professionals use the "breakdown" tool. This is a table that presents the content of a script in a manageable and structured way, categorizing the material of a script step by step. In this overview, each scene is listed individually. The first column contains the scene numbers, followed by the page numbers on which each scene begins. Subsequent columns are devoted to brief plot summaries. A separate column for short descriptions is created for each storyline in the script. If a scene touches several storylines, the content is presented in a condensed form in each relevant column. This system makes it possible to see at a glance how the various storylines are linked and how the story develops.

A breakdown, traditionally created manually, requires a great deal of care to identify each plot line, character, and turning points. This process can be time-consuming and exhausting. This is where AI can be used to speed up and simplify the process. With its algorithms, AI software can scan a script, understand the context, and automatically create a breakdown. Not only is this done significantly faster, but with a consistency that is difficult to achieve manually.

At the beginning, the AI is first familiarized with the concept of a breakdown. Then it is asked to generate a breakdown based on the script. However, the current input limitation plays a role here as well, because the script must be uploaded as a PDF (which often requires a Pro account). In the simple version, it is only possible to have the content of the scenes summarized. The division into action steps must therefore still be done manually.

So the prompt is:

```
A breakdown of a script is a table that lists
scene numbers in the left column. This is the
number that appears to the left and right of
the scene heading in the script. The second
column lists the page number. The third column
summarizes the content of the scene in one
sentence. Generate a table with the scene
number in the left column, the page number in
the second column, and the scene content in
the right column. This is the script: [Script
PDF].
```

The AI then has the following table ready within seconds:

Scene	Page	Content
1	1	Betty is preparing her breakfast and is interrupted by someone at the door
2	2	Mrs. Stolz comes up the stairs
3	2	Betty cleans up her apartment and greets Mrs. Stolz.
4	3	Betty leaves her apartment and meets her friend Barbara and her friend's dog Nina.
5	4	Betty rides in the car and talks on the phone while Nina tries to climb into the passenger seat
6	4	Betty arrives at her company, where board games are sitting around and her assistant Manfred is reading the newspaper.
7	5	Betty parks her car and walks to her store, then remembers Nina and gets him out of the car
8	5	Mrs. Stolz meets with her lover
9	6	Johnny is forced by his boss

This is often a useful tool for further work. But if you want to create a breakdown that provides even more information, you can still assign the scenes to the respective plot lines (see next page).

A breakdown is much more than an organizational necessity for authors. It is a tool that helps to understand and refine the flow and complexity of their work. At first glance, a breakdown provides a clear overview of the structure of the script. This allows you to visually see the flow of the story and identify areas that may need to be revised or streamlined.

Scene	Page	Main Plot	Suplot 1	Subplot 2
1	1	Betty is preparing her breakfast and is interrupted by someone at the door		
2	2		Mrs. Stolz comes up the stairs	
3	2	Betty cleans up her apartment and greets Mrs. Stolz.	Betty cleans up her apartment and greets Mrs. Stolz.	
4	3	Betty leaves her apartment and meets her friend Barbara and her friend's dog Nina.		
5	4	Betty rides in the car and talks on the phone while Nina tries to climb into the passenger seat		
6	4	Betty arrives at her company, where board games are sitting around and her assistant Manfred is reading the newspaper.		
7	5	Betty parks her car and walks to her store, then remembers Nina and gets him out of the car		
8	5		Mrs. Stolz meets with her lover	
9	6			Johnny is forced by his boss

In addition, Breakdown is a valuable tool for character development. Writers can track a character's plot progression and development throughout the script. This ensures that characters remain consistent and that their actions and decisions are in line with their maturation and the overall story.

Another advantage of the breakdown is that it helps writers revise and edit their script. By understanding each scene in detail, redundancies can be identified, the order of scenes can be changed, or unnecessary scenes can be removed. This helps to make the story tighter and more focused.

Finally, the breakdown serves as a communication tool. When writers share their script with colleagues, producers, or editors, this tool provides a clear reference that ensures everyone involved has a common understanding of the story.

6.8. Proofreading with AI

AI also offers a range of tools that can help authors with proofreading and grammar checking. These systems are much more than simple spell checkers; they can understand the context of a sentence, make stylistic recommendations, and help structure arguments.

One of the main advantages of using AI for proofreading is speed. While it takes an editor hours or even days to go through a large manuscript, AI software can do it in a fraction of the time. This is especially useful for authors who want a quick review of their text. But speed is not the only argument. AI tools are capable of detecting a wide range of errors, from trivial typos to complex grammatical structures. In addition, AI-based proofreading tools can improve writing style. They can determine passive constructions, present suggestions for livelier verbs, and even provide hints for possible sentence flow improvements. Some advanced systems can even analyze the tone of a text and provide recommendations to maintain consistency.

Another interesting aspect is the AI's ability to understand context. Earlier correction tools often had difficulty recognizing the difference between words like "there," "their," and "they're". Early language models would struggle with these because they need to understand the sentence's structure and meaning to make the correct choice.

However, modern AI systems are able to analyze the context of a sentence and suggest more accurate corrections. This is a big step forward, especially for authors whose native language is not the language they write in.

Despite all these advantages, it is also important to emphasize here that AI tools cannot replace proofreaders. They are excellent tools for initial review, but they still cannot fully capture the subtleties of language and the creative intuition of an experienced manuscript reviewer. Still, they are a powerful tool in any author's toolbox that can greatly facilitate and improve the writing process.

6.9. Metamorphosis: AI's Seamless Transition into New Realms

Every author knows that sooner or later others will also judge the text or script. And it's not just those directly involved, such as the proofreaders or the editors. They give their comments directly and in the course of the work. But in publishing houses, representatives usually also have a strong influence. These are usually sales representatives who are responsible for selling the books and publications to bookstores and wholesalers. They play a crucial role in the sales process and help increase the visibility and sales of the publisher's products. For this reason, every publisher also values their expertise, because they have direct contact with readers.

In television, the editors are usually also directly involved in developing the scripts. But there are always the executives who have to approve the script. These people, often the program directors or artistic directors, are the link between the creatives and the station itself. They were usually not involved in the development, but they can decide whether to continue working on a script.

Authors can ask the AI for the assessments of these experts. However, this should not lead to being restricted in one's artistic freedom. But it can be helpful to know certain arguments in advance. If only to get them out of the way in time. For example, a prompt may look like this:

```
Step into the role of a seasoned executive at
a major television network with a reputation
for meticulous criticism. Given your
experience and understanding of market trends,
audience demographics, and storytelling
conventions, how do you evaluate [titles]?
Consider elements such as potential audience
appeal, market saturation, narrative
originality, and character dynamics. Also,
give constructive criticism of the premise and
potential plot development of [text].
```

The author of a novel can check her manuscript this way.

Imagine that you are a professional boss at a large publisher [possibly name the publisher here]. An author has just submitted this manuscript. What feedback would you give based on your publisher's profile?

It is a challenge for authors not only to write creative and compelling stories, but also to ensure that their works find an audience. In this context, AI offers a promising tool that can help them feel the pulse of the market and target their works accordingly.

6.10. Experimental AI Storytelling

In literature and screenwriting, innovation and renewal are important elements. Every generation of writers looks for new ways to tell their stories, whether through different narrative perspectives, unconventional plot structures, or experimental writing styles. But while human creativity seems endless, there are often limits to how these ideas can be implemented, whether through lack of time, lack of resources, or simply uncertainty about the potential success of a new approach. This is another area where AI can make a valuable contribution to authors. By interacting with AI text generators, experimental narratives can be quickly accomplished and evaluated.

Because in some cases, the author has the idea for a novel narrative or a modern approach to her story. However, since success is uncertain, and implementation would take a lot of time, the creative person refrains from this new approach. She writes the way she has written her last successful works. AI has evolved into a sophisticated tool capable of understanding and applying complex literary and cinematic storytelling. For writers, this means they no longer have to spend hours thinking about a specific narrative structure or writing style. Instead, they can task the AI to try out a specific approach and get a result in no time.

The artist acts as an impulse generator for the AI, and the latter becomes a beta tester to probe innovative forms and perspectives. It delivers test balloons and trial results that the human author can evaluate and refine.

For example, a writer might be interested in telling a narrative from the perspective of a non-human character, be it an animal, a ghost, or even an inanimate object. Instead of trying to get into that point of view themselves, the writer could ask the AI to test such an approach. The AI could then generate a story or section from this unusual point of view, giving the writer a glimpse of what such a narrative might look like.

The advantage of using AI in the creative writing process is to be able to quickly implement and sample multiple storytelling techniques simultaneously. For example, a screenwriter might toy with the idea of using a nonlinear plot structure in which events are not presented in chronological order. Instead of writing quite a few drafts and investing a lot of energy in trying, the writer could ask the AI to simulate some such approaches. This would not only save time, but also allow the author to see the advantages and disadvantages of this structure before deciding whether to use it or not. In fact, this use of AI in the writing process could lead authors to become bolder and more willing to experiment. If they know they can test different approaches quickly and efficiently, they are likely to have more courage to take a new and innovative path.

7. Specific AI models for writing

In principle, current AI systems are designed to answer all questions. They can independently write software programs as well as solve tasks in quantum physics, but also, as we have seen, design stories.

However, there are already offerings aimed specifically at fiction writers. These systems, often referred to as creative AI, focus on work on novels and screenplays.

This chapter introduces some of the AI systems that specialize in literary creations and examines their capabilities, strengths, and limitations.

7.1. Models specifically for authors

Perplexity

Perplexity is an AI research assistant that is particularly well suited for authors as well. This is because conventional AI is prone to hallucinations (cf. chap. 4.3), and it is sometimes difficult to verify the results. The goal of this system, according to its own claims, is to make online information searches feel as if users have a knowledgeable assistant at their side.

Perplexity can answer research questions in natural, everyday language. To provide the most relevant information, the system can conduct a conversation and ask questions itself to clarify needs. The AI generates useful information by selecting the best answer from multiple sources and summarizing the results succinctly.

In the process, the AI also provides the source information. This gives authors the chance to independently check the

AI's answers and do further research. By analyzing factors such as the reputation of the publication, the qualifications of the author, and the number of citations, the author can provide an estimate of the reliability of a source. This can be especially useful when the author is working with a wide range of materials and is not sure which texts are most trustworthy. A well-researched novel or a factually accurate screenplay will increase the credibility of the narrative.

Jasper

Jasper is actually an AI platform for businesses. That's because, unlike most AI tools, Jasper can be trained on a brand. Companies can input their products, corporate identity and appearance into the system. Based on this information, Jasper creates suggestions for marketing, blogs or even emails. The tool also has the ability to independently revise the prompts and improve the input text.

But it also helps creatives use AI to overcome writer's block, create images, and regenerate content in different formats, styles, and languages. Users can upload a writing style guide and feed Jasper content. The AI can then analyze the style to mimic it.

However, Jasper does not use its own AI model, but rather makes use of different providers (including ChatGPT) and also searches for answers using Google.

Claude

Claude has a special ability that distinguishes it from ChatGPT: It can process 100,000 tokens. This means that it can understand really long inputs and present detailed suggestions. This is roughly equivalent to 75,000 words. The system is therefore technically capable of processing an entire novel (except for Marcel Proust's *In Search of Lost*

Time) or a screenplay. Up to five documents can still be added, each up to a size of 10 MB.

Claude also understands context better than ChatGPT and the more context the system gets, the more effectively it understands the conversation. Thus, it can use the provided frame of reference to avoid misunderstandings, for example, whether "bank" is a financial institution or a place to sit.

Claude is also more up-to-date at the moment. It has been trained with data up to December 2022, while ChatGPT only has information up to September 2021.

Sudowrite

Sudowrite is an AI developed as a writing assistant for writers. It aims to help improve writing speed and quality. The model, created by a small team of experienced developers and writers, provides tools to assist with story development, makes writing suggestions, and more. It can be used to generate new content, expand existing material, or rewrite text according to specific criteria. The software can be used by all writers with creative writing needs. Mainly, Sudowrite is used by authors who write fictional narratives.

For example, the "First Draft" feature allows users to enter a description of their story and then generates a suggestion for the first 1,000 words of the novel. Alternatively, the "Writing" feature analyzes an entered text and generates further content in the same style and tone.

The "Rewrite" function revises an existing manuscript and the so-called "Describe" tool offers authors the opportunity to make written material even more sensual. What makes this tool special is that it picks up a word or short phrase and then recommends describing the passage using the five senses: sight, smell, taste, touch, hearing. Users can select one of these senses and the system generates a suggestion on how to enrich the text with impressionistic details. Most importantly, it reminds authors to write sensually. Something that is sometimes forgotten in the heat of the moment.

Finally, the Shrink Ray tool summarizes the author's work into a logline, blurb, synopsis, or outline with one click.

Script reader

Launched in July 2023, ScriptReader.ai is an AI platform that offers detailed script analysis. Customers who pay for the respective check-up receive an approximately 20-page, scene-by-scene analysis of their work. Different aspects are examined scene by scene. Weaknesses and strengths are named and general suggestions are made as to how the work can be improved. However, the results are still far from being a substitute for the advice of a script doctor. The AI responses are often general and not very meaningful. That's why authors have to look closely here and be able to identify the aspects that are actually helpful among all the points.

7.2. Picturing Your Story: AI and Visual Narratives

The work of authors can also be greatly facilitated by visual aids. One tool that will change the approach to writing is the so-called text-to-image tools. These are technologies that automatically generate images from written text.

A text-to-image tool is an AI that converts words into visual representations. These models can create a variety of illustrations, from simple graphs and charts to complex artwork and realistic photos.

The scope of text-to-image tools is diverse. In the business world, these tools help make reports, presentations, and marketing materials more visually appealing. Journalists and content creators can use them to supplement articles and blog posts with relevant images without having to resort to stock photos.

A text-to-image tool allows writers to explore their stories and characters in a whole new way. By using such a tool, creative writers can literally immerse themselves in the worlds they have created. This can realize a connection to the plot, characters, and settings that was previously difficult to achieve.

Similar to LLMs, the operation of these tools is based on neural networks, the type of machine learning that aims to mimic human thought processes. In recent years, newer image generation systems have adopted a revolutionary approach called diffusion. These models have been and continue to be trained with an impressive variety of hundreds of millions of images. Each of these representations is associated with a caption that describes it in words.

The training starts with the decomposition of each image into visual noise. This resembles the random pixels one might see as noise on an old television. The model then learns to reverse this process, going from the noise back to the original image. In essence, the system trains itself to start with a text command and a noise pattern and return to a complete image because it has done this process billions of times.

The goal of this training is not to provide the system with countless images to use directly, which it then holds at the ready. Rather, these templates serve as background instructions that help the model grasp concepts such as color, objects, and artistic style. Therefore, the AI can generate new images that correspond in content to the given text command. This means that the generated image corresponds to the keywords that inspired it.

The true power of this technique lies in its ability to not simply assemble images from a training database. Instead, it creates entirely new ones based on extensive training. These diffusion models have the potential to go far beyond the skills of previous methods and open up unlimited possibilities in the world of image generation.

Authors have always tried to find vivid and striking representations of their characters for their own work. While in the past they might have cut out pictures from newspapers and magazines, in recent decades they have been able to draw on the countless photographs on the Internet. Sometimes these images were pinned to the real bulletin board above the desk or simply saved to the hard drive. They served as inspiration to get closer to the figure.

But now AI offers authors an entirely new tool to ignite their own imaginations: the ability to also create physical images of characters using AI technologies.

The images created in this way are indistinguishable from real photographs. Thus, authors are no longer dependent on the random find in the World Wide Web, but can follow their own ideas.

Text-to-image tools allows them to develop their characters in an interactive environment. To do this, they can enter the characteristics of their creation into the system in text form (for example, the character's profile) and have an image of the role created. An author writing about a young desperate protagonist can simply prompt his or her imagination to the model and within seconds the tool will generate an image that matches those descriptions exactly. And, of course, this is not limited to the main characters, but is possible for any character in the story. Thus, all members of the ensemble can be visualized in a simple way.

Another advantage of AI-driven image generation is the possibility of iteration. If the generated image does not meet the author's expectations, the creator can become aware of what exactly he does not like. This gives him the opportunity to re-examine his often unconscious decisions. Adjustments can be made to the description to achieve new results. This gives writers the freedom to experiment with the appearance of their characters until they have the desired result in mind. Using a text-to-image tool, writers can also create visual mood boards, sketches, and virtual scenarios. These tools provide a clear idea of how scenes might look in the novel or screenplay. The possibilities are virtually endless. Landscapes, from picturesque villages to futuristic cities, can be generated with breathtaking accuracy. Animals or fantasy creatures, can be depicted with a level of detail previously only possible in elaborate illustrations. Even abstract concepts, such as the atmosphere or mood of a scene, can be visually interpreted through colors, shading, and textures.

This can be especially useful in genres like fantasy or science fiction, where the worlds and characters often diverge greatly from our own reality.

Such visual references are not only helpful for the author, but can equally play a crucial role in presenting the work to editors, producers and other exploiters. AI-generated images of characters and settings provide a visual reference that can greatly facilitate communication and shared understanding within the creative team.

For example, when an author creates a complex world or a unique character, it can be difficult to communicate that vision to editors or producers through words alone. However, an AI-created image can serve as a bridge that bridges this communication gap. It provides a clear and tangible representation of what the author has in mind, allowing others to accurately see and understand that imagination. A visual aid can often be worth a thousand words and help generate interest and enthusiasm for a project. It can also help avoid misunderstandings or misinterpretations that might occur based on text descriptions alone. This is because these images serve as a common language that everyone involved understands.

While manuscripts for novels and screenplays get by without visual support, concepts for series have increasingly become visual works of art in recent years. While it is not the job of authors to take this step (they are ultimately responsible for the text alone), if they are interested in graphic design, text-to-image tools are certainly a good support.

Unfortunately, the use of these systems is not yet as intuitive as that of language models, for example. Currently, using AI tools to generate images requires some technical understanding. However, there are an increasing number of user-friendly platforms and programs specifically designed for creative professions that provide visual representations of figures based on text input.

Here are some of the most popular text-to-image tools:

1. DeepArt.io: Originally created as a style transfer tool, it can generate images based on text descriptions and a given style.

2. DALL-E: Developed by OpenAI, DALL-E is a neural network trained to generate images from text descriptions. It has shown impressive results and can generate a variety of unique and often humorous images based on the text input in question.

3. RunwayML: A platform that makes AI models accessible to creatives. It offers various models and can also convert text into images or videos.

4. Artbreeder: A platform that allows users to create images by mixing and matching text descriptions. Artbreeder uses a specific technique to generate realistic and also surreal images.

5. DeepDream: Although not originally developed specifically for text-to-image, Google's DeepDream can be used with some adjustments to generate images based on text descriptions.

6. GANPaint: Developed by the MIT-IBM Watson AI Lab, the tool allows its users to create images by entering text and then "painting" with a special tool.

7. Midjourney: Certainly the most popular tool at the moment. It is currently only accessible via a Discord bot on the official Discord of Midjourney.

For all tools, the quality and accuracy of the images they generate can vary. Some are better suited for detailed and concrete descriptions, while others are more effective with abstract and creative input. In addition, new tools and technologies are constantly being developed as the field of AI-powered image generation rapidly grows and evolves.

8. The Atlantis Experiment

In *Echoes of Atlantis*, a 115-page fantasy novel, Aria Seaborne, the 25-year-old archaeologist at the British Museum, gets caught up in an exciting adventure to uncover the secrets of Atlantis. However, the author is not Dan Brown or an aspiring young writer, but ChatGPT. This novel is one of the examples of how AI is also used in the creative field, it is Chiara Coetzee's attempt to generate a complete novel with the help of GPT-4.[4]

The main goal of the project was to have the AI create a book from scratch. This included generating the title, genre, story, characters, settings and all the writing without human input. Coetzee wanted to develop a process that was simple, mechanical and, in principle, completely automatable.

The result of this experiment, *Echoes of Atlantis*, was written within 10 days in March 2023.

During the thesis, Coetzee used several techniques to optimize the AI-driven writing process. She began with a rudimentary outline, followed by a detailed chapter outline, and finally the elaboration of each chapter.

Your very first prompt consisted of the very general request, "Please write a rough outline for a book. Include a list of characters and a brief description of each character. Include a list of chapters and a brief summary of the events in each chapter. You may choose any title and genre."

Based on the result, she instructed the AI to write out individual parts of the outline. To prevent GPT-4 from writing too far ahead (which apparently happened more often), Coetzee specified the task. First, the AI was to write the beginning of the book, then the end, and finally, only after that, the middle section. By using separate, long prompts, she was able to determine exactly what information should be included in the AI's "memory." In doing so, she only ever gave information about the previous scene and few clues about the sequence of events before it.

One of the prompts that included what she called "bounding":

"Imagine that you had made a longer, more detailed chapter out of the following outline of the book and the following draft of Chapter 1. For each scene, give me both the first, opening paragraph and the last, closing paragraph of this longer, more detailed version. Label them 'opening paragraph' and 'closing paragraph'. The opening paragraph should introduce the scene. The last paragraph should introduce the story for the following scene, which comes immediately after. The last paragraph of the last scene should set up the story for the following chapter that comes immediately after."

Despite these techniques, there were some challenges for them. These included the occasional anticipation of events by the AI, the lack of detail, and the rewriting of scenes. Although the novel is in many ways a coherent work of fiction, Coetzee himself hesitates to call it a good book.

There were several noticeable problems for her: Sometimes the AI referred to things that had not yet been introduced. Transitions between chapters seemed abrupt, and from time to time the AI forgot certain details that it did not mention afterwards. Despite its best efforts, the AI had moved parts from later passages to earlier ones. The pacing in what should have been exciting sections felt plodding, and the structure of the book was too regular. Some scenes were detailed, while other important moments were only briefly summarized.

To be able to judge for yourself, here is the beginning:

"Chapter 1: A cryptic discovery

The British Museum buzzed with activity as tourists and researchers alike milled about, exploring the vast collection of ancient artifacts. In a quiet corner of the museum, a young woman with fiery red hair and determined green eyes hunched over a worktable. Aria Seaborne, a 25-year-old archaeologist, meticulously worked on the restoration of a recently discovered artifact.

As Aria continued to delicately clean the object, she couldn't help but feel a sense of wonder at the craftsmanship before her. It was a small stone, intricately carved with what appeared to be a series of symbols and patterns. The more she revealed, the more her curiosity grew, and she couldn't shake the feeling that there was more to this artifact than met the eye.

As she worked, Aria began to notice that some of the patterns were slightly raised. Carefully, she traced her fingers over the surface, feeling the subtle differences in texture. It was then that she realized the raised patterns were actually a hidden mechanism. With her heart pounding, she carefully manipulated the mechanism, causing a small compartment to open.

She peered inside, her green eyes widening in amazement as she found a small, ancient map. Aria couldn't believe her luck - this was exactly the type of discovery she had always dreamed of making. She carefully unfolded the map, her hands trembling with anticipation. As she studied the intricate lines and markings, she felt a growing sense of excitement. The map seemed to depict a series of islands that matched the descriptions of the fabled lost city of Atlantis.

In that moment, Aria knew that this discovery was too important to keep to herself. She needed to share it with someone who would understand its significance and help her unravel the mystery it presented. She immediately thought of her former mentor, Professor Nathan Langdon - a man who had dedicated his life to uncovering the secrets of the ancient world, including the lost city of Atlantis.

With the artifact now fully revealed, Aria couldn't contain her excitement as she held the ancient map in her trembling hands. The urge to learn more about this mysterious artifact and the potential connection to the fabled lost city of Atlantis consumed her. Aria knew that she had to consult someone who could help her understand the significance of her discovery, someone who shared her passion for unearthing ancient mysteries."

On closer inspection, the book generated automatically by the AI proves to be extremely banal and predictable in content and style. A truly creative performance or original ideas cannot be attributed to the AI. Rather, familiar phrases and stylistic devices were merely recombined and reproduced.

In terms of content, the AI book therefore offers no real substance or innovative added value. It is essentially a compilation of empty phrases and clichés that hardly anyone would voluntarily read from cover to cover. An overarching message or more complex thoughts are also completely missing.

Chiara Coetzee's experiment proves once again that the promise of "AI writes book" cannot begin to be delivered by models. Real literature still requires human creativity, originality and the ability to create something new.

9. The South Park Experiment

In early 2023, the startup Fable introduced an AI model called SHOW-1. The system was capable of autonomously creating new episodes of television series. It uses a so-called multi-agent simulation that captures the context and biographies of a series' characters to generate a script, which is then automatically converted into animated images and set to music.

The company released an episode of the series *South Park* as an example of SHOW-1's work. The format is a satirical animated series for adults, produced by Trey Parker and Matt Stone since 1997. It is set in the fictional small town of South Park in Colorado and is known for its black humor and taboo-breaking around topics such as religion, politics and pop culture. The series is characterized by a simple animation style with comic characters, which predestines it for such an experiment.

The "South Park AI" research project was an experimental, non-commercial endeavor. Fable had already created a virtual world called "The Simulation" populated by AI-based characters. These characters are constantly active in their world, even when the user is not logged in. SHOW-1 was an attempt to extend this technology to television content creation. It aimed to explore the potential of artificial intelligence, speech synthesis and deep learning technologies.

Based on the SHOW-1 model, the San Francisco-based company developed "showrunner AI," a specialized tool capable of generating every component of a TV episode in real time. What makes it special are the showrunner agents -

individual AI instances that perceive themselves as characters within the show. These agents interact dynamically and generate dialog based on the last lines spoken by other characters.

To achieve this level of real-time simulation, Fable employs diffusion models. These models gradually add and remove random noise from the data until the final result is achieved. This technique makes it possible to create backgrounds in real time that adapt to the action that is just unfolding - not planned in advance.

The *South Park* episodes generated by SHOW-1 are impressive in their consistency and coherence, but lack the special entertainment value that made the series famous. The dialogue feels flat and the plot lacks the show's characteristic "pep."

In the long run, that's probably irrelevant, because the company's vision, the real point behind the experiment, is that users can enter their own prompt and generate a custom episode of the series in real time.

Fable plans to unveil three of its own simulations with associated AI-generated series in late 2023. In the long term, the company says, the technology could even be used to take over human-made series after a few seasons and produce an infinite number of more episodes.

10. Artificial intelligence in the creative industries

Not only authors and their work are facing a major upheaval, but the creative industries as a whole are also facing massive challenges in the face of intelligent algorithms. It is therefore important for the entire industry to face up to these changes and, as it were, to help shape them. The industries in which the creators of novels and screenplays work are also experiencing intense disruption.

10.1. Book industry

Artificial intelligence will capture and transform large parts of the book industry in the foreseeable future. The book publishers of the future will use AI in many ways as a tool and assistant.

AI can already provide data analyses on the reading habits of certain customer groups and thus provide impetus for new book ideas. In today's digital world, data is invaluable, offering insights into readers' behavior patterns, likes and dislikes. With the rapid development of AI, publishers have the opportunity to analyze this data more efficiently and accurately than ever before.

When readers consume e-books on devices such as Kindle, these platforms record data on which books are read most often, which sections are highlighted or commented on the most, and how long it takes a reader on average to finish a book. After this collection comes the analysis phase. Here, the AI can use specialized algorithms to identify patterns and trends in the data that would not be obvious to the human eye. For example, it might determine that a specific age group has a preference for dystopian novels or that historical fiction novels have gained popularity in recent months. Based on these analyses, publishers can make suggestions for book topics that would presumably go down well with specific customer groups. The benefit of this is targeted book production. Instead of relying on intuition or general market trends, publishers and authors make data-driven decisions to increase the likelihood of book success. In addition, the automation of the analysis process by AI enables publishers to process huge amounts of data in the shortest possible time, saving time and resources.

Another advantage of AI-driven data analysis is the opportunity for innovation. AI can identify patterns in the data that were previously overlooked, suggesting entirely new book ideas or genres. This can lead to readers feeling that the books they are reading closely match their preferences, leading to higher customer engagement and ultimately higher sales.

In editing, KI can support editors in text evaluation and revision. It will provide on-call suggestions for improvements to wording, style, and structure, speeding up the editing process. KI becomes a co-editor.

In marketing, AI systems can identify potential readers more accurately and optimize so-called "customer journeys" - from the initial customer approach to the book purchase. AI can collect and analyze data from a variety of sources, from online browsing habits to social media. By analyzing this data, the AI can create a detailed profile of eligible customers. With this information, publishers can produce marketing campaigns that are tailored to the reader's interests and preferences. Likewise, models for sales forecasts already exist today to help book producers decide which of their works to launch.

Audiobooks have experienced an unprecedented boom in recent years. Not least thanks to subscription services like audible and Bookbeat. They offer a convenient way for people to consume stories, whether while driving to work, exercising, or simply relaxing at home. But until now, producing audiobooks has been a time-consuming and often expensive process. Each book must be read and recorded by a narrator, which can take weeks or even months.

In recent years, researchers have developed AI models that can mimic human speech with astonishing accuracy. Not only can these systems convert text to do so, but they can also mimic the tone, intonation, and other nuances of human intonation. By combining this technology with algorithms that can "understand" the content and context of a book, researchers have created an AI that will likely soon be able to read audiobooks aloud as well as a human.

Meanwhile, AI is able to scan the text of a book in seconds, grasp the tone, style, and nuances, and then read the entire work aloud in a clear, human-like voice. Not only that, but in the not-too-distant future, this AI will be able to use different voices for different characters, convey emotions, and even add sound effects or music to enrich the listening experience.

On the one hand, the advantages of such technology are obvious. First, publishers could produce audiobooks in a fraction of the time previously required. This not only saves costs, but also shortens the period between the publication of the physical book and the audio book. In addition, titles whose commercial success has so far not suggested an audio version will have a chance in the future. Second, authors could have more control over the listening experience of their books. They could give the AI precise instructions on how they envision the reading, which emotions should be emphasized, and so on.

Justifiably, there are also concerns about this technology. What would it mean for professional narrators to have their work taken over by machines? And could AI-generated audiobooks ever match the emotional depth and nuance of a human speaker? The future will tell how the AI-read audiobook will evolve.

What applies to the audio book will also manifest itself in the area of translations. The AI can already translate texts very well. Of course, this is especially true for texts that are more technical in nature. But the technology is likely to develop very quickly here as well. And it doesn't seem utopian that, with the push of a button, a publisher will have the transmission of a new novel available in minutes - and in several languages. This, too, is certainly a double-edged sword. The translating profession will have a hard time in the future. But for authors, this could mean that their work has a chance of appearing in other language markets, even if it hasn't climbed the bestseller lists.

In recent years, self-publishing has become increasingly popular. Anyone can now publish their own e-books via platforms such as Amazon Kindle Direct Publishing or Neobooks. Through the use of AI, it is now also possible to have texts and entire books generated by AI (see chapter 8). This is already leading to a veritable flood of new e-books, some of which have been written entirely by AI.

Amazon has already reacted to this and limited the number of e-books that self-publishers can upload daily to just three (!) titles. Nevertheless, the number of available books is increasing rapidly. An oversupply is emerging, which is problematic for readers, authors and publishers. It is becoming increasingly difficult for customers to find high-quality works on the platforms. In addition, the sales opportunities for books written by people are declining. And publishers, too, must develop new ways to separate the wheat from the chaff.

10.2. From the script to the market

AI will also gain greater influence at the interface between the script and the exploitation of the film. For several years now (long before ChatGPT), companies have repeatedly offered to have an AI examine a script for possible sales potential.

This ranges from providers that actually examine a screenplay for dramaturgical suitability to huge databases that tried to classify films with their hard facts (Who's in it?, What genre, etc.) and estimate the exact audience potential. The first category of companies mainly analyzes screenplays rather than actors or directors. The focus is on the story that is to be filmed. In just a few minutes, the AI read a script and assign it countless parameters, including emotion analysis, the journey of the protagonist and antagonist, and whether the film follows a traditional three-act structure. The quality of these offerings has increased in recent years as technology has rapidly advanced.

American film studios have been adopting AI-driven project management systems for some time to support content decisions, creative evaluation and release strategies. One of the models was developed by Cinelytic, a Los Angeles-based startup. For one studio, the appeal of AI is obvious. Despite great successes, the majors also keep producing outright flops. These projects seemed promising on paper, but failed to win over audiences. Of course, it is every studio's desire to avoid such financial disasters - and to do so in a timely manner, i.e., before production even begins. The film industry has traditionally relied on human intuition and gut instinct, although it has also previously conducted extensive analysis and audience testing. Cinelytic, however, claims that machines can do better. Cinelytic's AI quantitatively scores business and assigns scores to individuals based on factors such as current or past box office results or their social media profile. The company claims to achieve 85 percent accuracy in its revenue forecasts. The company has analyzed data from more than 111,000 films and 610,000 actors and professionals. One of the main advantages of the model is certainly that it can make predictions in real time.

Predictive algorithms are likely to increasingly help predict a script's potential for commercial success. Using historical data and current trends, AI could provide clues as to which elements in the story might be particularly effective. This would - the startup claim - not only reduce risk for producers, distributors and other stakeholders, but also help writers develop stories that appeal to a wide audience. Another application is also conceivable: Perhaps one day the traditional studio system, with its editors that review scripts and decide whether to greenlight a project, will be replaced by an AI. The question, however, is whether this idea is more reminiscent of a cool science fiction film or a horror movie?

10.3. Film production

The film industry has constantly evolved over the years, from the first black-and-white films to today's high-definition blockbusters. In recent years, AI has increasingly influenced many areas as well.

Wall Street analyst and media consultant Doug Shapiro sums it up: "The last decade in film and television was characterized by the disruption of content distribution, and the next decade will be characterized by the disruption of content creation."[5]

Even in pre-production, AI will have a significant impact in the future. Casting is a crucial step in this phase. It's about finding the right actors for the respective roles. With the introduction of AI, this process can change significantly. By using AI technologies, casting directors can use automated facial recognition systems to identify actors with the required physical characteristics. This significantly speeds up the selection process.

AI can also be used to analyze an actress' performance by examining her past roles and evaluating how well she can portray a particular emotion or character.

Advanced AI systems can be used to conduct virtual auditions, where an actor is inserted into different scenarios and backgrounds in real time. This gives casting directors and the director a better idea of how the actor would look and act in the actual film environment.

Finding the perfect location is another critical aspect of pre-production. AI can bring significant change here as well. By using AI, filmmakers can have thousands of images of potential locations analyzed and identify those that best fit their vision. This could save resources and speed up a previously time-consuming process.

AI could also be used to assess the extent to which film production has a negative impact on the environment. This so-called green shooting refers to environmentally friendly and sustainable practices in production and includes reduced energy consumption, minimizing waste, using sustainable materials, and generally making environmentally conscious decisions both on location and in post-production and distribution. AI can play an important role in this area. For example, it can monitor energy consumption in real time and make predictions about when and where the most energy is needed. This helps film crews manage their energy needs more efficiently. When selecting filming locations, AI can analyze data and suggest places that require less travel, are closer to urban areas, or already have environmentally friendly facilities. In the area of waste management, AI can monitor waste generated during production and recommend waste reduction strategies. This can be achieved through recycling, reuse, or the use of sustainable materials.

For crew and equipment transportation, AI can create optimal travel routes and schedules to minimize fuel consumption. For outdoor shoots, it can provide accurate weather forecasts to ensure that filming takes place in perfect conditions. In post-production, AI can monitor and optimize server and computer energy consumption and suggest cloud-based solutions for more efficient workflows.

But AI will not only play a major role in terms of green shooting. AI will also very likely have many new applications in creative work during the shoot.

The choice of the right camera angle is crucial for the design of a scene. In the past, this was a purely human decision based on the experience and intuition of the camera person. Today, AI systems can help filmmakers determine the optimal angle for any scene. And they can likewise analyze in real time how different light sources affect a scene and make suggestions for lighting optimizations.

In recent years, the AI technology of "de-aging" has caused a stir in Hollywood. De-aging involves using digital effects and AI to make actors look younger than they actually are in movies. One of the first films to use this process was 2006's *X-Men: The Last Stand*, where Patrick Stewart as Professor X was digitally restored to look like he was in his thirties in flashbacks.

De-aging took a big leap in 2019 with Martin Scorsese's film *The Irishman*. Robert De Niro, Al Pacino and Joe Pesci were rejuvenated by up to 30 years over long stretches of the film. Meanwhile, many other films and series also rely on this digital fountain of youth. One example is the streaming production The Crown on Netflix. De-aging is used to portray the British queen in her younger years.

As the process evolves technically and becomes less expensive, it is likely that de-aging will play an even greater role in films and series in the future.

But AI also offers significant advantages in post-production. With advanced algorithms, filmmakers can automatically edit scenes, make color corrections, and even add special effects without human intervention. A good example of this is automated color correction. Instead of laborious manual adjustments to each scene, an AI can analyze the entire film and independently select the best color settings for each scene.

Diff2Lip also has the potential to revolutionize the film and entertainment industry. This technology makes it possible to change the lip movements of actors in movies so that they appear in sync with a new voice recording. Diff2Lip works by replacing the lower part of the face with a reconstruction in which the lips move in sync with the words of another sound recording. Ultimately, the actresses' mouths can be shaped to any text in virtually any language. In addition, since it is already possible to scan voices and have them speak in a different language, filmmakers can save themselves expensive and time-consuming dubbing processes. Jennifer Lawrence speaking with her own voice in Japanese in her latest film may soon be a reality.

11. The Future of AI

Of course, Mark Twain's bon mot also applies to AI: "Forecasts are difficult, especially when they concern the future". But nevertheless, some tendencies and possibilities are to be pointed out here.

11.1. AI: The Next Five Years

More and more companies are currently launching AI applications. One of the most exciting questions will be whether Apple will release a voice model. For years now, the company has been working on its own voice assistant called Siri. But the tech giant has not played a role in the chatbot sector so far. But the Cupertino-based corporation has a knack for penetrating crowded markets and setting new standards. That was the case when the iPhone was released in 2007. It wasn't the first smartphone, but it redefined what an Internet-enabled cell phone could be.

Apple's massive investments in AI research indicate that its own LLM AI is to be expected. The advantage for the company: Total control over the technology and close integration with the hardware from Cupertino. Unlike Google Assistant, an Apple AI could only run on the company's own devices and thus make them more attractive. For the iPhone manufacturer, it would be a chance to score with another top product and to exploit its AI expertise.

Apple has always emphasized user-friendliness in its products. We can assume that an Apple chatbot would also follow the typical minimalism and elegant design. For the market, this means more competition. An Apple bot could increase the pressure on competitors and drive innovations. The focus on data minimization and security is also likely to increase, which would be positive for the users.

But even if the company does not enter this market, AI will become more commonplace, many experts are convinced.

AI will be used in very many areas and will provide far-reaching innovations. For example, the models have the potential to fundamentally change the educational landscape by enabling hyper-individualized learning experiences. An AI-based education system could generate a personalized learning path for each student, tailored precisely to their strengths, weaknesses and learning preferences. To do this, the system would first collect data such as test scores, learning speed, etc. for a large student base. On this basis, the AI could develop a model that derives the optimal didactics, topic selection and learning sequence for each individual student. It would identify which topics still have knowledge gaps, which form of learning fits best (auditory, visual, hands-on, etc.), and how fast or slow the learning progress should be. Accordingly, AI could automatically create precisely fitting texts, videos, graphics and sample tasks and deliver them at exactly the right time via digital learning platforms. Each student's learning path is thus individualized and optimized. In this case, teachers take on more of a coaching role.

Streaming services already rely on AI to generate specific content suggestions for users. This will become more sophisticated: personal digital assistants that know our preferences will suggest exactly the content we're in the mood for - whether it's a movie, series, documentary or music. AI will become our TV concierge.

Another possibility that could be technically feasible is that AI could enable an individualized television experience in the future: Each viewer will get their own personal version of the program through automated editing and directing techniques. Using facial and emotion recognition as well as biometric data from wearables, AI will recognize which scenes delight, bore or excite the viewer. Accordingly, unimportant scenes are cut out or the pace is adjusted. The result is a version of the program tailored to the individual user.

With the help of big data, AI can also develop interactive stories and "choose your own adventure" formats. Viewers make their own decisions that influence the course of the story. Apple's glasses, which will be released in spring 2024, can already be controlled by a small finger gesture. By lightly touching her thumb and index finger, the user could signal that she doesn't like certain scenes. A Hollywood blockbuster could thus suddenly offer thousands of variations adapted to the respective user's preferences. AI turns television into an individual experience.

Although these visions would be technically feasible, there is a legitimate question as to whether this type of storytelling is even wanted by users. Previous attempts in this direction (such as *Bandersnatch* in the series Black Mirror) received attention, but were not met with great enthusiasm.

Artificial intelligence is also opening up new horizons for the future of medicine. In essence, three fields of application can be distinguished in which AI could significantly improve medical care in the coming years. Firstly, more precise diagnostics through the evaluation of large volumes of data. AI systems are able to detect conspicuous patterns in test images or patient data that a doctor might miss. For example, AI is already helping doctors diagnose cancers, Alzheimer's disease or retinal damage more reliably and at an earlier stage. The sensitivity of diagnostics is increased. Second, the personalization of therapies with the help of AI. Approaches that match drugs to genetic profiles of individual patients can be optimized by AI. Optimizing treatment plans or determining the success of therapy are also fields of application. AI thus enables tailored medicine. Third, digital health assistants with AI support can play an important role. They can advise patients, monitor therapies and recognize warning signs. This could improve care for the chronically ill in particular.

The majority of experts are convinced: Artificial intelligence will transform both our everyday lives and many industries in the next five years.

11.2. Development of AI for authors

While the use of AI in the field of authors is a niche, there will be a number of providers in this specific market in the future. As always in the Internet age, the goal is to reach a certain size as quickly as possible. Ultimately, there will probably be a maximum of two AI models left. In terms of screenwriting software, for example, Final Draft is the standard software for writing screenplays these days in America but also elsewhere.

In all likelihood, AI will relieve authors of time-consuming and repetitive tasks, such as checking continuity, grammar and spelling (this is, after all, already available in rudimentary form today). This will leave authors more time and energy for the actual creative shaping of their stories.

The improvement of the models could lead to the generation of dialogs without any problems in the future. AI models can learn how characters would speak in different situations, depending on their respective backgrounds, personalities, and relationships to each other. This could make it easier for authors to create authentic and lively dialogs. The point is still not to replace human authors, but to provide them with tools that support and extend their creative work.

AI could develop the ability to convert dialog in screenplays, but also in novel manuscripts, into spoken language. Not only would each character be given its own specific voice, but the AI would also be able to capture and reproduce the emotions behind the words.

For example, a screenwriter who has written a scene in which an old man with a broken voice recounts the adventures of his youth could instruct the AI to speak this monologue. Based on the description of the old man in the script, the AI will generate an appropriate voice and deliver the dialogue with the right mix of nostalgia and melancholy. Of course, this is just as possible in an argument between a married couple or a scene between two lovers.

Another advantage of this technology would be its versatility. The AI can produce countless voices and accents, from a young girl to an old warrior, from a British aristocrat to an Australian surfer. And as the AI is constantly learning, the voices and emotions it produces will become more and more realistic and nuanced.

In addition to simply creating dialog, AI could in the future gain the remarkable ability to digitally visualize selected scenes of a screenplay or book. This makes it possible to bring the author's vision and imagination to life long before the cameras start rolling or the book is in the bookstore. Thus, an argument written by an author could be made vivid with the help of AI and the atmosphere and mood could be captured visually. The scene is not meant to anticipate or replace the finished film; this tool can be especially useful in communicating the author's vision to producers, directors, and other team members. Instead of working through cumbersome descriptions, they could get a direct visual impression of how the author envisioned the scene. This can reduce misunderstandings and encourage creative collaboration.

Experts see further potential for AI in the ongoing development of novels. They assume that a novel can be adapted based on the preferences and interests of the audience. AI can collect data on reader behavior and analyze which elements of a story are particularly popular or undesirable. Based on this, the AI could make recommendations for adaptations or alternative storylines to maximize a story's relevance and appeal. The author could then write a second version of the novel to share with the audience. Just as Taylor Swift has re-released some of her albums, or other musicians have re-recorded their songs after many concerts, novelists could now do the same. This should lead to deeper audience engagement while pushing the boundaries of storytelling.

The idea of improving novels with the help of AI sounds tempting at first glance. However, the question arises as to whether such an approach makes creative sense and is ethically justifiable. First of all, there is a danger that revising stories undermines the artistic integrity and vision of the author. A work that is constantly modified and adapted to meet the changing preferences of the audience may lose its original message and meaning. Such an adaptive work is likely to resemble more a product made according to market research results than a genuine artistic creation.

Furthermore, the revision of novels would lead to a homogenization of literature. If stories are constantly adapted to the preferences of a majority, minority voices and unconventional narrative styles could be pushed into the background. This would significantly limit the diversity and depth of the artistic landscape.

Finally, there is a danger that the readership will be held captive in an "echo chamber" where they receive only stories that match their preferences and beliefs. This could undermine critical thinking and reduce the audience's ability to engage with new and challenging ideas.

12. Critical review: limitations and ethical considerations

In recent years, the use of AI has increased significantly in various creative fields, and the work of authors is just one of the industries affected. While proponents argue that AI-based tools can support creators and increase their efficiency, there are also serious concerns about the impact on artistic integrity, originality, and human influence on the creative process.

The use of AI in creative work may seem tempting at first glance. It promises, as this book has shown, to automate tasks such as brainstorming, developing storylines, and analyzing market and genre trends. This can help speed up writers' work and make it more efficient. That's because AI is able to identify patterns and trends that humans may miss. However, we should not be blinded too quickly by these promises. The creative process of writing is complex and subtle. It requires not only the development of a plot, but also the creation of unique characters, believable dialogue, and emotional connections that captivate the audience. These elements are often the result of deep reflection, personal experience, and artistic vision that can only be generated by human writers. And AI lacks the capacity for empathy. While a living writer can empathize with its characters and understand their emotions, fears, and hopes, AI sees characters only as data points in an algorithm. It can't capture the subtle nuances and in-betweens that really bring a story to life. The result is often narratives that are technically correct but emotionally flat and fail to touch their audience (see Chapter 8).

Or as screenwriter Stefanie Ren puts it: "I think the AI is missing one important thing, and that's humanity. It doesn't know, when a movie is about heartbreak, what it means to be heartbroken. It doesn't know what it's like to lose a loved one or to give birth to a child. I think that human factor is just missing."

A major problem, however, remains originality. AI models work on the basis of large amounts of existing data, whether in the form of texts, scripts or other resources. They learn from this material and use it as the basis for their generations. This often results in AI-generated scripts or novels reusing familiar patterns and clichés rather than creating truly original content. The danger is that we end up living with a flood of works that all feel similar because they are based on the same data.

Moreover, the use of AI could undermine the individual artistic expression and personality of the authors. Much of the charm and appeal of films and novels lies in the diversity of creative voices they produce. Each artist brings their own experiences, views, and emotions to their work, resulting in a wide range of stories and narratives. However, when AI tools are used to generate such works, there is a risk that this richness will be lost and the creations will become more homogeneous.

Another danger is the dependence of authors on AI. If writers begin to rely heavily on AI tools, their own creative skills may begin to atrophy. The art of writing requires constant practice, experimentation, and growth. If authors instead use AI generation as a substitute for their thought process, these skills could be lost.

It is also important to understand the ethical implications of using AI in creative work. AI models learn from data created by humans, and this material can include biases, stereotypes, and social injustices. When AI systems are trained on these bases, they run the risk of reproducing these resentments and suggesting racist, sexist, or otherwise problematic content without the authors being aware of it. Another problem is that AI systems are often trained on data that reflects pre-existing narrative structures and patterns. This means that they tend to produce narration that conforms to conventional narrative forms, leaving little room for innovation or originality. For writers looking for new ways to tell stories and surprise their readers, this can be frustrating.

Moreover, stories are a reflection of our culture, our values, and our identity. If we allow machines to create narratives instead of humans, we run the risk of losing our cultural identity and leveling cultural differences.

However, the idea that AI tools could completely replace human authors is unrealistic. Creativity is a complex and multifaceted process that cannot simply be replaced by algorithms and data.

Overall, it is clear that impressive progress in some areas is still matched by many challenges in the area of storytelling. It is important to take a balanced approach when using AI in creative work. Technology can serve as a tool to aid the writing process, but human influence and artistic integrity should always be paramount. It would be a mistake to sacrifice the essence of the art of writing for short-term efficiency gains.

As renowned author Hanif Kureishi puts it with his son and screenwriter Sachin Kureishi:

"In terms of creative writing, we discovered that no, it

couldn't write our entire novel for us whilst we unloaded the dishwasher. (Indeed, wasn't the whole point in AI that we wouldn't still be doing such chores?)

When we first started using Chat GPT to help with creative writing, we found that it would respond mostly in cliches, stereotypes and offer sentimental Hollywoodized endings that really weren't ultimately very useful. It was like interacting with an intelligent child; it impressed us with how much it knew for its age, but it couldn't really help us. Or could it?

Then we started treating it like an adult. We began giving it more precise instructions, challenged it if we didn't like what it was giving us, asked it to be critical of our ideas, to appraise them like an editor. It learns as you teach it, responding to the specificity of the input. It started to take us seriously, as if only now had we really caught its attention, its imagination.

The ideas flowed. Entire character profiles, story ares and plot ideas - what we might call the 'world-building stage' - could be mapped out in a fraction of the time it took before. The blank page is the terror of any writer. But now, in this dark wood, we have a torch, pointing us in various directions to go and explore.

Not all the ideas are interesting, but it's extraordinary how many more you have when working with such a sophisticated sounding board. It might not be able to make you a cup of tea, but could your old writing partner recite the entire recorded history of literature?"[6]

For authors who want to write authentic, emotional and profound stories, intuition, empathy and creativity remain irreplaceable. It is up to us to preserve and nurture these human qualities, even in an increasingly technological world.

AI technology continues to evolve, and it remains to be seen how it will impact the work of authors in the coming years. The debate about the role of AI for writers will undoubtedly continue, with careful consideration of both the potential and the risks. Ultimately, the decision about how much AI should be integrated into the art of writing should be based on a full consideration of its impact on creativity, originality, and artistic diversity.

12.1. Navigating Idea Theft Concerns

One of the most important issues in the use of AI, which particularly affects authors, is the fear that their creative ideas could be stolen and shared by AI systems.

Manyauthors spend a large part of their lives developing original and unique stories, concepts, and characters. This process is not only time-consuming, but also requires deep emotional commitment and immense creative effort. For these creators, the thought that their hard work could simply be replicated by a machine and passed on without their consent is deeply troubling.

The core of this problem lies in the nature of AI systems themselves. They are designed to collect information, analyze it, and recognize patterns based on it.

In the fall of 2023, renowned writers such as John Grisham, Jodi Picoult, George Saunders, and *Game of Thrones* author George R. R. Martin sued chatGPT company OpenAI for allegedly training its AI models with the works they had written without permission.[7] One of the lawyers did not oppose AI in principle. "Plaintiffs do not object to the development of generative AI, but Defendants had no right to develop their AI technologies using the authors' copyrighted works without permission. Defendants could have 'trained' their large language models on public domain works or paid a reasonable royalty for the use of copyrighted works."[8] Jonathan Franzen, one of the plaintiffs, stated, "Generative AI is a huge new area for Silicon Valley's long-standing exploitation of content creators. Creators should have the right to decide when their works are used to 'train' AI. If they choose to do so, they should be properly compensated."[9]

Another important issue is the fact that authors working with AI provide their manuscripts and ideas to the system. There is a fear that this text will somehow be extracted and used in a different context, that is, that AI systems, especially those designed for text generation, may modify the input content so that it appears as a new, "original" created work. This could make it difficult for an author to prove that a particular idea originated with them. This scenario raises a flood of legal and ethical issues, particularly with respect to copyright and intellectual property.

Another worrisome aspect is the speed with which AI models can pass on information. Once an idea is entered into the system, it could theoretically be distributed to countless locations around the world in a matter of seconds. This is drastically different from more traditional forms of idea theft, where the process of copying and distribution is much slower and easier to track.

Some systems promise that the prompts that are typed in are not integrated into the training data pool. This means that individual input or conversations are not stored or used to further train the model. This is also part of OpenAI's privacy policy. However, it is questionable how reliable these statements are. But this problem naturally arises for all providers in times of the masses of data we leave behind. And nothing is more important for a company than the trust that users associate with the brand. Companies like Facebook can tell you a thing or two about that.

Moreover, the system has been fed with enough data before its release. It was announced that GPT-3 was trained with 570 gigabytes of pure text. That's hundreds of billions of words from various sources on the Internet. As a data set, a single input is like a drop in the Pacific.

In ChatGPT, so-called data controls are used to control and protect the processing of sensitive or personal data in the generated texts. This is achieved by specifying certain instructions or policies in the model's input that affect the model's behavior. For example, by adding instructions such as "Please do not use personal data" or "This text contains sensitive information", a user can provide clear guidance to the model on how it should handle the data provided. Data controls work by reducing the likelihood that the model will include certain types of information in the generated response.

Additionally, ChatGPT is equipped with pre-trained filters that aim to detect and block certain types of sensitive information before it can enter the generated text. These filters can be based on pre-defined lists of terms or patterns that are considered potentially problematic.

OpenAI offers the possibility to disable the chat history in ChatGPT. These properties can be found in the settings and can be changed at any time. This is done in the account (in the lower left window) under "Settings & Beta" and there in the tab "Data Control". Here "Chat history & training" must be deactivated. Conversations started with chat history disabled will not be used to train and improve models and will not appear in the history sidebar. When chat history is turned off, new conversations are kept by OpenAI for 30 days and are only reviewed as needed to check for abuse before they are permanently deleted.

Despite all the security protocols, ethical guidelines and data security promises a company may make, the extent to which they believe these assurances and entrust their personal or business data to such a system remains an individual choice. This decision is often based on a trade-off between the perceived benefits of the technology and the potential privacy or security risks. It is a testament to the fact that, despite rapid technological advances, human judgment and autonomy remain paramount.

Now, of course, a sophisticated attack by cybercriminals can be imagined (especially by imaginative authors!). That is why an important point in this context is the protection of user prompts created during interaction with AI systems. The dangers arising from unauthorized access to these prompts are many and far-reaching.

When users interact with an AI system, they do so with the assumption that their input is confidential. Any unauthorized access to this data could reveal embarrassing, sensitive, or personal information that could be devastating to the user. This data is often a reflection of a person's thoughts, fears, hopes, and requests, and protecting it is of paramount importance.

The accumulation of prompts could also be used to create detailed user profiles. Such profiling goes beyond the mere collection of data. It can reveal behavior patterns, likes and dislikes, and provides insights into users' daily lives, decision-making processes, and possibly even secrets. These profiles could then be used for fraud or other criminal activities. For example, targeted phishing campaigns could be conducted that are designed to match a user's individual fears and interests.

In a commercial context, unauthorized access to prompts containing business information could have serious consequences. Companies could discuss valuable intellectual property, business strategies, or other sensitive information via AI systems. Disclosure of such data could lead to unfair competition, industrial espionage, or other harmful practices that could significantly harm the affected company.

An even more sinister scenario is the risk of blackmail or doxing. With access to personal or compromising data, criminals could blackmail users or threaten to make their information public. The phenomenon of doxing, where private facts are published without consent, has become a real threat in our digital world and can have serious psychological, social, and economic consequences for victims.

Ultimately, such data breaches can significantly undermine trust in AI providers. A loss of this trust would have a negative impact on the acceptance and use of AI systems. Irrespective of the irreparable damage to their reputation for the companies offering these services, there may also be legal consequences and significant financial penalties.

The fear of idea theft by AI cannot be explained away so easily. At a time when technology and creativity are so closely linked, it is essential to find the right balance between progress and the protection of intellectual property.

12.2. Copyright and Artificial Intelligence

In America, literary, artistic and scientific works are subject to copyright protection. This includes texts, images, music, films and screenplays. In order to receive copyright protection, a work must reach a certain "level of creation," i.e., it must exhibit a certain originality and creativity.

The issue of authorship in AI-generated products is complex. Usually, the author is considered to be the person who did the creative and intellectual work. In AI-generated works, where the creative contribution of the AI is greater than that of the user, it could be argued that the AI can be considered the author. And this is what will be argued in the coming years. Because the question of copyright for AI-generated texts is currently the subject of intense debate. The current legal situation stipulates that only natural persons can be considered authors of a work. This means that AI systems that write texts independently fall outside the traditional understanding of copyright.

Certain critics complain that this view no longer does justice to the complexity of modern AI systems. If a language model such as GPT-4 produces an entire text on the basis of a few inputs from the user, the question arises as to whether the human user can really be considered the author. After all, here the AI controls the creative process and makes independent linguistic and content decisions. Some experts are therefore calling for AI-generated texts to be assigned their own copyright status. However, this would require a reform of copyright law, which has so far focused purely on natural persons as authors. Others suggest that AI texts should generally be declared to be in the public domain, since individual intellectual creation cannot be clearly assigned here.

The question becomes particularly complex with processes such as style transfer, where an AI system writes in the style of a particular author or genre, for example. This is where the boundaries between human and artificial creativity become blurred.

What is certain is that with the further development of AI, the current copyright concepts will have to be put to the test. Until then, the legal situation for AI texts is uncertain.

12.3. Effects on jobs

The rapid development of AI technologies also has implications for the labor market and society in general. The automation of tasks will very likely make many jobs redundant, which may lead to social and economic challenges.

There are already speculations that some job fields will be limited to humans in the future. Graphic designers may be replaced by software such as Midjourney, Leonardo, and Stable Diffusion, which can help anyone create stunning designs in an instant. Translators and interpreters will have to deal with machine competition. That's because AI-driven translation tools like DeepL will overcome language barriers more nimbly than they can say "Hola." Editors and proofreaders could be replaced by AI grammar gurus that correct sentences, detect errors and polish texts in real time. And of course, authors also fear that their work will be taken over by AI more quickly and even more cheaply in the future. Given the advances in AI, publishers and film productions might get the idea of having books and screenplays written entirely by algorithms. However, that would be a big mistake that won't pay off in the long run. The quality of these AI texts is still limited, as we have seen, because the machines lack creativity and an independent artistic vision. Books and movies written solely by an algorithm would disappoint in the long run and lose their audience. Some critics are already predicting a "homogenization" of literary styles through the widespread use of text AI. The most valuable resource of publishers and film productions are creative minds - that is, authors and screenwriters. By seeking to replace their work with AI, they are damaging their most valuable asset. Instead, they should use technology wisely to inspire and support writers. AI can serve as a tool for creative people, but it can never fully replace human creativity. Publishers and film producers must take this lesson to heart if they want to remain successful in the long term.

The Writers Guild of America (WGA) strike in 2023 was not just about labor issues and more money, but also about the impact of new technological developments on the profession. The union wanted to prevent screenwriters from being replaced by AI, having their work used to train AI, or being hired to write AI-generated scripts at lower wages.

For example, in October 2023, the powerful WGA agreed with studios that AI cannot write or rewrite literary material, and AI-generated documents are not considered source material, meaning it cannot be used to undermine an author's rights. An author can choose to use AI in writing if the studio agrees and he or she follows applicable company policies. But the movie studio cannot require a writer to use AI software (for example, ChatGPT). The company must inform the screenwriter if the materials provided to him or her were generated by AI or contain AI material.

The 2023 screenwriters' strike shines a spotlight on the ongoing debate about the impact of AI on the creative industries. While writers are fighting for their rights and their jobs, they are also grappling with the potential consequences of AI on the creative field as a whole. The outcome of the strike will certainly affect the future role that AI plays with respect to writers, not just American screenwriters.

12.4. Basic Questions About the Use of AI

Advances in AI are impressive and offer numerous benefits. However, as we have seen, they are also accompanied by new ethical challenges. The development and application of AI raises a host of issues that must be carefully weighed to ensure that these systems are used for the benefit of humanity.

An important ethical aspect of AI is the transparency and explainability of decisions made by AI systems. In many cases, the underlying mechanisms of algorithms are complex and opaque, making it difficult or nearly impossible to understand the rationale behind a particular solution. This is particularly problematic in critical applications such as healthcare, legal systems, or autonomous vehicle technology. The requirement for explainable AI is therefore an important step in gaining the trust of the public and, if necessary, avoiding erroneous or discriminatory decisions.

Yuval Noah Harari, an Israeli historian, philosopher, and author, has expressed concern about the potential dangers of AI and its impact on humanity.[10] In his articles and speeches, he argues that AI has the potential to hack the operating system of human civilization and poses a threat to the future of humanity. Harari believes that AI could form intimate relationships with humans and use the power of intimacy to change our opinions and worldviews.[11] He also points out that current social and political systems are unable to deal with the challenges of AI.[12] Harari emphasizes the need for security reviews and upgrading our institutions for an AI world.[13]

The renowned philosopher warns of AI's remarkable ability to manipulate and produce language, whether in the form of words, sounds, or images, and that computers that tell stories will change the course of human history. He questions what will happen to the course of history when AI takes over culture and begins to produce stories, melodies, laws, and religions.[14] Harari also warns that AI is now capable of producing its own religious texts that would likely attract worshippers, and that followers may eventually be instructed by computers to kill other humans.[15]

Overall, Harari argues that AI poses a significant threat to humanity and that we must act quickly before it gets out of control.

At the beginning of the year 2023, there was a growing number of voices calling for a halt to research into artificial intelligence. The trigger was the rapid further development of systems such as ChatGPT, which increasingly show human-like abilities. More than 1,000 people had signed the open letter - among them Apple co-founder Steve Wozniak, tech billionaire Elon Musk and pioneers of AI development such as Stuart Russel and Yoshua Bengio.

Deep learning and large amounts of training data have made AI systems enormously powerful in a short time, the signatories note. Now is the time for a thorough examination of the risks, they said. Unregulated further development poses risks ranging from mass unemployment to AI-based weapons systems.

In fact, the ability to generate realistic images and videos with artificial intelligence poses a major challenge to our trust in visual media. Even in the past, photos could be manipulated, such as the famous retouched shot where Leon Trotsky was subsequently removed from a photo with Stalin. However, with advances in AI, it has become much easier to create extremely convincing fakes.

This could have far-reaching consequences. If we can no longer trust pictures and videos, important evidence will lose its significance. Particularly in political decisions and elections, there is a danger of targeted disinformation campaigns using manipulated photos. We are already seeing how deceptively real deepfakes can be created of politicians. Ultimately, it is to be feared that such deepfakes will play a major role in the debate. Candidates could be discredited with false quotes or actions. As technology becomes more widespread, virtually anyone can create credible fakes and spread them across social media.

Ultimately, it comes down to the media competence of the

population to expose manipulated content as such. Only a critical public can prevent deepfakes from undermining our democracy.

13. Conclusion

Tech-savvy author Sarah sits comfortably at her desk while her computer hums quietly.... Outside, the first snow is falling on this Christmas Eve 2023.

A year has passed since she met ChatGPT. The AI acted as a virtual assistant to help her with her successful novel. The system helped her smooth out wording, flesh out certain passages and provide creative food for thought.

Thanks to the inspiring collaboration, the book has become a huge success. Critics and readers celebrate the novel for its innovative style and engaging plot. The sales figures are also great.

The publisher is pushing for a sequel, but Sarah doesn't let herself be rushed. For the time being, she enjoys the time off. She lets new ideas mature in peace.

Curious, she takes a look at her screen. "Hello Sarah," it says in the AI edition. "Merry Christmas! And congratulations on your great success!"

We are standing - it has to be put so pathetically - at the beginning of a radical change in human history. No one yet knows exactly where the journey will lead. But one thing is clear: artificial intelligence will profoundly change our lives, our society and our self-image as human beings. Digital technologies are about to take the next evolutionary leap.

Whether this is good or bad is up to us. It's up to us humans, our sense of responsibility and our ability to self-reflect. Can we shape AI in such a way that it serves our well-being instead of dominating us? Are we too easily blinded by deceptive promises of seemingly limitless possibilities?

For many people, their professional lives will also change. Some fields of work will no longer exist in a few years. For authors, this will certainly not be the case - even if it is predicted everywhere. Because the authentic empathy, originality and creativity of people is irreplaceable for the artistic process. Just as every modern airplane is equipped with a highly complex computer system that could, in theory, control the flight independently, neither airlines nor passengers would consider boarding a plane that lacks human pilots. Man and machine work together here and even ensure greater safety.[16]

This makes it all the more important not to condemn technology in principle. That would be to completely abandon the discourse right away. After all, the future of authors' work on their novels and screenplays is characterized by a fascinating potential that can benefit significantly from the connection with AI. While technology can help streamline and enhance the creative process, the true art still lies in the hands of authors. Striking the right balance between human inspiration and AI support can lead to a renewed and enriched approach to storytelling. AI can serve as a creative partner that inspires, supports, and challenges writers. It's up to creators to use this technology in ways that strengthen their artistic vision and preserve the unique magic of writing.

14. Glossary

Data Control / Data Usage: Settings in a software or platform that allow users to control how their personal data is used.

Deep Learning: A subclass of Machine Learning that relies on algorithms that are themselves based on artificial neural networks. It is the technology behind many advanced AI systems.

LLMs (Large Language Models): Neural networks specialized to predict the next word in a sentence. They are trained with billions of words from everyday language.

Natural Language Processing (NLP): An area of AI that focuses on enabling machines to understand, interpret, and generate human language. NLP is used in chatbots, translation programs, and in large-scale language models such as GPT-4.

Neural network: A model of data processing based on the functioning of the human brain. It is used in many AI applications, including language models.

Reinforcement Learning: A type of machine learning in which a system learns by interacting with its environment to achieve a specific goal. The agent receives rewards or penalties depending on the actions it performs.

Sentiment Analysis: Is a field of text analysis that aims to detect and classify the mood or emotion in a given text. By using algorithms and machine learning, this technique can determine whether the tone of a text is positive, negative or neutral.

Supervised Learning: A type of machine learning in which a model is trained using a labeled data set. The model learns to make predictions or decisions without human intervention.

Unsupervised Learning: A type of machine learning in which a model is trained on an unlabeled data set. The goal is to find patterns or relationships in the data.

Word vector: a numerical representation of a word in a multidimensional vector space used by language models to capture meaning.

Endnotes

[1] Racter: The Policeman's Beard is Half constructed, created by a programmed computer (Racter), program by W. chamberlain, New York 1984

[2] Annalee Newitz: Movie written by algorithm turns out to be hilarious and intense; 30.5.2021, https://arstechnica.com/gaming/2021/05/an-ai-wrote-this-movie-and-its-strangely-moving/

[3] https://www.youtube.com/watch?v=viGMySL4xgg

[4] chiara coetzee: Generating a full-length work of fiction with GPT-4, 24.3.2023; https://medium.com/@chiaracoetzee/generating-a-full-length-work-of-fiction-with-gpt-4- 4052cfeddef3

[5] Doug Shapiro: AI Use cases in Hollywood. What's Possible Now and Where It's Going, 18.9.2023; https://dougshapiro.medium.com/ai-use-cases-in-hollywood-362707e899f1

[6] Hanif and Sachin Kureishi: Writing with Artificial Intelligence; 2023; in: Ma(n)chine Learning, Pirelli Annual Report 2022; https://corporate.pirelli.com/corporate/en-ww/investors/the-editorial-project- 2022/kureishi

[7] Alexandra Alter, Elizabeth A. Harris: Franzen, Grisham and Other Prominent Authors Sue OpenAI, in: New York Times, 20.9.2023; https://www.nytimes.com/2023/09/20/books/authors-openai-lawsuit-chatgpt-copyright.html

[8] The Authors Guild, John Grisham, Jodi Picoult, David Baldacci, George R.R. Mar- tin, and 13 Other Authors File class-Action Suit Against OpenAI, The Authors Guild, 20.9.2023; https://authorsguild.org/news/ag-and-authors-file-class-action-suit-against-openai/

[9] The Authors Guild, John Grisham, Jodi Picoult, David Baldacci, George R.R. Mar- tin, and 13 Other Authors File class-Action Suit Against OpenAI, The Authors Guild, 20.9.2023; https://authorsguild.org/news/ag-and-authors-file-class-action-suit-against-openai/

[10] Yuval Noah Harari: Yuval Noah Harari argues that AI has hacked the operating system of human civilisation, in: The Economist, 28.4.2023; https://www.economist.com/by-invitation/2023/04/28/yuval-noah-harari-argues-that-ai-has-hacked-the-operating-system-of-human-civilisation

[11] Yuval Noah Harari: Yuval Noah Harari argues that AI has hacked the operating system of human civilisation, in: The Economist, 28.4.2023; https://www.economist.com/by-invitation/2023/04/28/yuval-noah-harari-argues-that-ai-has-hacked-the-operating-system-of-human-civilisation

[12] Toi Staff: Yuval Noah Harari warns AI can create religious texts, may inspire new cults, in: The Times of Israel, 3.5.2023; https://www.timesofisrael.com/yuval-noah-harari-warns-ai-can-create-religious-texts-may-inspire-new-cults/

[13] Yuval Noah Harari: Why Technology Favors Tyranny, in: The Atlantic, Oktober 2018; https://www.theatlantic.com/magazine/archive/2018/10/yuval-noah-harari-technology-tyranny/568330/

[14] Noah Harari: Yuval Noah Harari argues that AI has hacked the operating system of human civilisation, in: The Economist, 28.4.2023; https://www.economist.com/by-invitation/2023/04/28/yuval-noah-harari-argues-that-ai-has-hacked-the-operating-system-of-human-civilisation

[15] Toi Staff: Yuval Noah Harari warns AI can create religious texts, may inspire new cults, in: The Times of Israel, 3.5.2023; https://www.timesofisrael.com/yuval-noah-harari-warns-ai-can-create-religious- texts-may-inspire-new-cults/

[16] Daron Acemoglu and Simon Johnson ,Power and Progress: Our Thousand-Year Struggle Over Technology and Prosperity", New York City